D0987631

RECOVERY
of HOPE

RECOVERY
of HOPE

Fifteen couples tell their experiences with
Recovery of Hope—intensive counseling for
marriages which seem beyond help.

NAOMI & JOHN LEDERACH

Good Books®

Intercourse, PA 17534

Design by Dawn J. Ranck

RECOVERY OF HOPE
Copyright © 1991 by Good Books, Intercourse, PA 17534
International Standard Book Number: 1-56148-046-0
Library of Congress Catalog Card Number: 91-74057

Library of Congress-in-Publication Data
Lederach, Naomi.
         Recovery of hope / Naomi and John Lederach
                  p. cm.
         Includes bibliographical references and index.
         ISBN 1-56148-046-0 : $11.95
         1. Marital psychotherapy—Case studies. I. Lederach, John.
II. Title.
RC488.5.L43 1991
616.89'156—dc20

                                                      91-74057
                                                      CIP

All rights reserved. Printed in the United States of America. No
part of this book may be reproduced in any manner, except for brief
quotations in critical articles or reviews, without permission.

Table of Contents

I
What is "Recovery of Hope?"

"It's the gap between what-might-have-been, and what is, that causes me such despair," Stuart explains, sizing up his marriage. "This 'partnership' is paralyzed and going nowhere. It's dead."

"That's the one thing we agree on," adds Martha. "What's more, I feel even worse about myself."

This disillusioned couple calls their earliest dreams fantasies and they are cynical about their hopes that mates should make each other happy and meet each other's needs. They've tried insisting that their spouses change. Each may have looked outside the marriage for someone else. What they are left holding instead is anger and resentment, loneliness and fear, blame and helplessness. Many couples acknowledge reality at this point and dissolve their marriage.

Recovery of Hope has dared to intervene at this moment and suggest that not all may be lost. In fact, the program specializes in working with those couples who have come to complete despair.

"I remember telling our counselor that our marriage is dead," recalls one veteran of Recovery of Hope. "Instead of trying to revive it, she replied, 'That's a good place to begin. Assume the old marriage is dead and start building a new one.' While I was startled, I also realized that I didn't want our old marriage. We were not asked to dismiss all the history that had been part of that marriage experience. But by acknowledging that there was no life in that relationship we found a place to begin again, and hope."

Two primary features distinguish Recovery of Hope from other modalities of therapy. First, couples seeking help are asked in an introductory session to listen to the stories of three couples who, like themselves, had come to the end of trying and hoping. Each "presenting couple," through a unique series of events, entered Recovery of Hope and eventually decided to continue their marriage, but on new footings.

Second, couples who choose to seek help beyond the introductory session enter a week of intensive marital therapy. Spouses who are experiencing great difficulties and intense conflict often find it nearly impossible to bring about change through weekly or monthly one-hour appointments. So much happens between counseling times that it is difficult to get to the heart of the issues. A consecutive five-day session can more effectively unearth trouble and build toward healing.

The Stories

Stories engage all of us powerfully in ways that no other words, teaching or information can. While stories of marital distress are full of shadows and pain, stories of true marital healing, can become instigators of hope within others. "Presenting couples" tell the truths of their lives—the discovery of their personal histories, the ravaging turmoil between them, their steps toward healthier partnerships, the strenuous demands of maintaining that health.

In these stories hurting couples may hear something familiar that parallels their own experiences. At the least they learn they are not alone in their suffering. They may even find courage— not magically—but with hard work to risk again. Hearing that others looked squarely at despair, yet chose the discomfort and possibility of working at change, can enliven the smallest notion of hope.

Presenting couples are not therapists. They are a touchstone of identification, a sort of reference point for struggling couples willing to be called beyond their hurt to healing. Presenters model ways to claim their histories, then weave them, along with new understandings, into promising futures together.

To have hope again is risky. Any of us about to undertake a new venture wants the promise that we will be successful. Most of us, having failed once and considering a second try, need a double assurance of success. But there are no such assurances. One must finally take a leap of faith. A remarkable number of couples choose to risk that leap as they listen to others, who have known little or no hope, share their stories. Many hurting couples become willing to begin new stories.

The Intensive Week of Marital Therapy

Marital despair requires concentrated and extensive attention. Recovery of Hope asks a major commitment from those couples who seek help beyond the Saturday morning introductory meetings. They must leave their homes, children, jobs and other responsibilities and spend Monday through Friday working exclusively on their marriages.

Recovery of Hope provides a home (bed and breakfast) for the couple in therapy, free of charge. In fact, these host homes are a supporting element throughout the week. They are couples chosen for their graciousness, whose children no longer live at home. They have good marriages and so are reinforcing role models, simply because of who they are. They accept the visiting couple without judgment or advice. They are volunteers committed to providing a comfortable setting where a couple can work at their difficult task. They are not "mini–therapists" and do not become involved in the couple's problems, but they do support them in many ways. They are pledged to confidentiality. Many couples stay in touch with their hosts for years—a benefit to both.

Therapists at the Recovery of Hope centers are usually husband–wife teams. Couples spend most of the week in co–therapy, although, depending upon the situations, they may also engage in considerable individual work.

The therapists take the first two days to assess where the couple's problems lie, what the issues are—from each spouse's point of view, as well as from their own. They use several psychological assessment tools to look at the differences, similarities and other issues that may emerge which would indicate deeper problems needing attention.

Together they spend several hours with therapists on a genogram, discovering the dynamics in each one's family of origin, their differences and similarities, and the expectations that each brought to the marriage. These genograms become "living documents" for the remainder of the week, reference points for new insights.

Each evening the couple is given assignments, designed and determined by what their needs are perceived to be. The homework varies from writing projects to reading articles and books together, to practicing communication skills to activities of many kinds.

The couple spends one morning session in psychodrama with two staff persons, the psychodramatist and therapists. Psychodrama is a method designed to deal with problems through action rather than through verbal discussion or talk therapy, which occupies most of the week.

In a warm–up period, the couple is invited to talk briefly about what brought them to Recovery of Hope and what they see as important issues between them. The director of the drama then sets up scenes, using staff persons to act out or reenact with broad strokes, situations that either have occurred or could have happened in the couple's life. One director recently explained, "It's like going to a play, only the drama shows scenes from your own lives so you can get a picture or image of the dynamics in your relationship."

Psychodrama can assist persons to *feel* the unfinished issues from their pasts or help them deal with current choices or decisions they need to make. The therapy team may alter the couple's circumstances from reality to permit them to try out new kinds of behaviors or interpersonal experiences. The couple has no script to follow, and their participation requires less acting skill than willingness to try to understand their own and each other's feelings and relationships. The exercise becomes another piece in the puzzle of assessment and treatment.

As the week progresses the therapists continue to work at assessment, gaining insight, understanding what has gotten in the way of a satisfying relationship, and discovering what changes each spouse would like to make and will need to make if the relationship is to work. During this time the staff also teaches skills in communication, negotiation, problem-solving, and relating in new ways so that the couple can allow new feelings to emerge. The specific design of the week takes shape according to each couple's needs and the issues that become apparent as the week moves along. Ultimately, Recovery of Hope provides a safe environment where hard issues can be brought up and dealt with in a sustained way.

If a couple gets into trouble with each other, falling back into their old patterns, they can try out their new skills or admit they're stuck and come back the next day to work together again with their therapists. It is positive and reassuring to know you will be assisted in dealing with your difficult times right away.

This intensive week of marital therapy creates another powerful dynamic. Each partner invests significant time, money and careful arranging to work without distraction on their marriage. It is an indication of some commitment on each one's part even if one of them is reluctant or even resistant to being there, which is not unusual. This sizable investment provides an impetus to make the most of their time in counseling, regardless of the outcome of the week.

By the end of the week, if the couple chooses to commit themselves to rebuilding their marriage, the therapists and couple together draw up a contract outlining the quite specific changes the couple has to make. This process in itself allows husband and wife to test the new skills they are learning. The contract builds in the couple's accountability to each other and to those who will see them in follow–up. It is a rather formal–looking document which all sign. The couple takes one copy with them; the therapists keep a copy. The contract becomes "grist for the mill" as the couple finds new ways of relating. But it can also be changed to meet their current needs.

If spouses choose not to continue their marriage, either at the end of the week or later, Recovery of Hope assists them in separating, trying to minimize the trauma. The staff helps them remember and celebrate their good times, grieve over their lost dreams and expectations, and experience the pain and disappointment caused by the demise of their marriage. The therapists mediate, as much as possible, the details of what needs to follow, such as their relationship to their children, home and belongings, and how to talk with family and friends in ways that are not destructive to each other. The staff also recommends that they explore the possibility of professional mediation services which are now available in many communities, if there are issues which require further attention.

Follow-up for further counseling and continuing support is crucial. A week, however good it may have been, is not enough. It may have provided a way of getting unstuck; it may have brought new insight, new commitments and even change, but a couple whose marriage is in serious trouble needs on-going support, either in therapy, or with their pastor, priest or rabbi. They need someone who will continue to assist them as they work at sustaining new behaviors and change, someone to whom they can go for help and to whom they can be accountable. They *will* fall into old patterns and traps. The real world inevitably tests the validity of their experiences during the intensive week. Although Recovery of Hope staff tries to prepare them for re-entry, it remains a difficult time for most couples.

While other innovative and successful marital therapy programs exist, Recovery of Hope developed with its unique aspects under the auspices of several mental health hospitals operated by the Mennonite church. Consequently, the therapists who work within the program, and the treatment design itself, place high value on nurturing the spiritual part of life. Recovery of Hope staff believe that personal faith in God enhances one's ability to recover from one's dysfunctional background and/or marriage. A personal faith in God does not shield one from hurt or damage, but it can encourage healing and growth.

Recovery of Hope does not screen its clients according to their religious preferences. The staff has observed, however, that persons who give some credence to religious faith find the program more helpful than those who don't.

Many of the stories in this collection contain references to God. These reflect the personal understanding of the storyteller.

This Collection

The personal stories in this collection are true. The names of the couples and other possibly distinguishing information have been changed to protect their identities.

These stories are somewhat representative of the hundreds of couples who have found the beginning of recovery in their telling. While many couples' experiences have common aspects, each is unique. That, too, is true of this collection.

2

I'll Stay With You But Don't Expect Anything

Matt and Susan tell their story regularly to other hurting couples at the Saturday morning introductory Recovery of Hope sessions. As one of the "presenting couples," Matt and Susan write their story so they are sure to say what they still find difficult to talk about, yet is likely to be helpful to those who have come in despair. These presentations are vulnerable. They express aloud and truthfully the pain these couples have known, usually much like that being experienced by their audiences. In contrast to their audiences, however, these "presenting couples" have discovered hope.

The format for the presentations is set: the couple begins their story with an introduction which the husband reads. Then, in alternating fashion, they tell of their journey, each spouse recounting the difficulty and hopelessness each has experienced. During the second half they again take turns, describing how they began to have hope for their relationship, and what they learned and worked at to make their marriage more satisfying. The wife reads a conclusion to their presentation.

Matt and Susan's story is presented here as they give it on a Saturday morning to inquiring couples. Matt begins.

"We are here today because we believe that there is hope for your marriage. We did not believe in that hope when we sat in your place one Saturday morning. We could not look at each other in love; only with disgust, anger and resentment. Our journey has not been an easy one. The pain of a broken relationship is healed through communication and time. We are not proud of what has happened; quite the opposite. We share it only so you, too, may find hope.

"We were young when we married. I was 20 and ready for the fun of marriage. What it became was hard, laborious work for which I was not prepared. I was not prepared for all that Susan expected. I grew up in a home where we just lived from day to day. The most exciting thing we discussed was the weather. You just lived. You didn't talk about living. Here I was with a wife who thought we should discuss everything. I would simply respond, 'I didn't really think about that,' or 'I don't know what I think about that.' She would often stomp away in anger and I would let her go. 'She'll get over it,' I would say to myself.

"As long as she was working full-time, things seemed to go okay, but when our first child was born, I realized that this baby would change more than just our sleep patterns! Financially the crunch hit me hard. I felt like the only solution was to take on more hours at work. So began the long 12-hour days that became such a big part of the last seven years.

"I would come home and not want to be bothered by anything. I just wanted to be left alone. Work became my sole purpose in life. I would often leave at 5:30 a.m. and work until 7:00 or 8:00 at night. I thought I was being a good husband, a good provider. Isn't that what a husband is supposed to do—provide security for the family? Actually, I was avoiding my home life.

"Sometimes Susan would ask me specific questions when I got home from work, or bring me a problem she was having with the children. I would often say, 'I'll think about it,' or 'Do whatever you want.' Then I would go sit in my chair, lift my newspaper as a shield and hide behind it. Susan would get angry and go watch TV. Things only got worse."

Susan gives her side of the story.

"I had a mother who taught me how to cook, sew and clean. I believed that was what I needed to know before getting married. In addition, I was in Future Homemakers of America, I took 4-H every summer and I even had a Marriage and Family class in college.

"Even though I wasn't sure Matt was *the* one, he was a nice guy, I knew I could have done a lot worse, and no one else was interested in me. So it seemed right. I imagined adoring a loving husband who would come home to me, make love and adore me in return.

"As weeks turned into months, my fantasies about marriage lay like all the crumbled Kleenexes beside our bed. Matt didn't seem to think about much at all! I would start discussions only to have them end with, 'Let me think about it,' but most of the time he never responded to what I had asked.

"I began to feel deceived and betrayed, but mostly I felt sorry for myself. At work I found the discussions, the affirmation, the real sense of personhood that I needed so much. I knew I was okay because of the way my co-workers responded to me.

"During my first pregnancy I felt wholeness too. I was going to be responsible for this precious gift from God. I was overjoyed and felt that things were going to be fine again. But five weeks after Eric was born, my world again began to tumble. The work of having a new baby was tremendous. Matt didn't seem to see any way he could help care for the baby. Occasionally he held Eric while he continued to read the paper. He did not wake up at night for feedings or even offer to change the baby. He was functioning in the only way he knew, having learned from his father who thought babies were women's work."

Matt says that he spent more and more time at work and eventually found companionship with a "certain female" with whom he worked. "I looked forward to work and found it increasingly difficult to be at home where things were only getting worse.

"I started taking off by myself on mini-vacations. I decided if I had extra vacation days, I was going to use them myself—I had earned them. I even tried to make sure that there was something to do by myself on Saturdays. I slept to avoid going somewhere or doing anything with Susan and the children. I would often sleep late on Sunday mornings so I wouldn't have to go to church. I began to think about how nice it would be to leave Susan and move somewhere by myself so I wouldn't have to be responsible to anyone but me.

"Things grew steadily worse. It took too much effort to talk with Susan about our troubles. If I suggested that the dishes needed to be washed or rattled the hangers in my closet searching for clothes I wanted, Susan would stomp away in complete outrage, as though I had criticized her. I didn't respond to her innuendos that I assumed no responsibility around the house and that I had no faith because I didn't attend church regularly. The wall between us kept getting higher. We were pushing each other as far away as possible, instead of seeing what we each needed to do to make things better."

Susan continues. "I spent a lot of time trying to ease my incredible hurt. I busied myself with babysitting up to eight preschoolers at a time for long periods of the day. Full of noise and the chores of children, I had little time to think of what I saw as failure on my part and the loneliness and depression I felt. I became extremely involved in church and community activities. I went to P.T.A., taught Sunday School, planned activities for community children, took meals to anyone who was moving in or out of the area or to families with a new baby. Each time I had a negative experience or felt as though someone did not seem to appreciate all I was doing, I knew that I was a failure and of no use to anyone.

"During dessert one evening Matt commented about the number of calories in the second piece of pie I was taking. To me it wasn't just a comment; it meant he thought I was fat, sloppy and disgusting. I fell apart from his smallest criticism or suggestions. I was convinced I had to be perfect! I would inquire about what Matt was doing at work, checking for whatever was substituting for our lack of relationship. He would assure me of his love and continue to work, sleep, work, sleep—and talk very little.

"I avoided looking at myself in the mirror because I couldn't face what I felt. Feelings of extreme failure flooded over me frequently. I knew Matt was avoiding any kind of conflict. He neither criticized nor encouraged me. The newspaper became a wall made of concrete. He expressed his need for time alone and yearly took several mini-vacations, excitedly packing to golf or hunt, oblivious to my stress in caring for two small children and the house. Once when he was gone Eric got sick and I was up repeatedly during the night. Then the kitchen water pipe burst and I knew I was the responsible one. I had to be.

"My martyr complex was developing solidly. I was the good one doing all the right things. I was certainly *not* to blame and it was time people knew what an awful life I was experiencing. I didn't tell anyone directly; I just stopped covering for Matt's absences and for his attitudes. I reveled in anyone speaking negatively about him.

"I knew our love was gone. But I decided I would remain in the marriage because that was my commitment. I knew, also, that I would never again love him. From here on out I would go through the motions, life would never be different and I would just be strong enough to endure it all. I decided to be single. I was a single parent anyway.

"I began making my own decisions about everything. I made purchases without consulting Matt. I was gone when I wanted to be gone, even if it was over suppertime. I believed that this separate life could lead me to better feelings about myself. In fact, it only served to darken my life. God seemed so far away. How was this possible? I decided to tell Matt that I would remain faithful to my marriage commitment, but I was leaving for a while so that I wouldn't feel so completely overwhelmed by the hopelessness of it all."

"One night after a particularly long day at work," Matt recalls, "Susan asked me if I had given any thought to what we had discussed the day before. I didn't answer her but went straight for my paper. She came over, took the paper, leaving me to feel fully exposed, and said emphatically, 'Don't be surprised if you come home some day and find that the children and I are not here anymore!' Even after she said that I didn't say a word. I retrieved the paper and went right on reading. Of course, I wasn't reading. I was thinking about what she said and I knew she was serious.

"The next day at work was a long one for me. I was uptight and edgy. I snapped at people. But I did leave work at a decent time, which was unusual for me. When I got home, Susan's car was not in the driveway. I walked into the house and it looked

Recovery of Hope

the same as when I had left in the morning; there were no toys lying around and it looked as though no one had been there all day. I panicked: 'Oh, no, she left with the kids!'

"I quickly ran up to the bedrooms and saw that everything looked normal, but I still didn't know what might have happened. About an hour later, much to my relief, I heard her car turn into the driveway. I said nothing. I sat reading the paper, showing no signs of what I was feeling.

"A day or so later Susan told me she had talked to our pastor. He suggested that we go to Recovery of Hope. I knew our marriage was miserable, but was it that bad? I wasn't sure I wanted to go. I didn't want people to know we weren't getting along.

"The next day at work I began to think about how good it would feel to be in love again with Susan. Maybe we should get some professional help in a safe setting. I told her that night that I would go. It felt like the right move.

"The introductory meeting was frightening. As we sat with other hurting couples, the silence in the room was deafening. The room felt cold, but sweat was running down my back.

"As the presenting couples started telling their stories, I felt as though they were telling my story—our story. We were on that same unloving road. I identified with much that they said.

"After their presentations, we had time to ourselves and then with a counselor to decide whether or not to try Recovery of Hope's intensive week of marital therapy. I still had doubts. Were we making too much of our situation? Couldn't we solve this ourselves? Would people at work understand why I needed time off? How could I explain it?

"We talked very little as we drove to Philhaven to begin our week. When we got there we simply sat in the car a while, not really wanting to go in. Finally, I got out of the car and began the journey. Susan followed.

"As the week progressed, we realized how long it had been since we just talked, and it felt good. But there was so much to see about ourselves, and that wasn't easy. The second day was the most difficult for me. With the help of several therapists, we saw our marriage in a new light. Using role play, they accurately showed us what a typical evening was like at our house. I didn't want to believe it! I told them I didn't act that badly.

"Our week took shape around two major points: understanding how we had come to be the way we were, and beginning to discover how we might resolve some of the difficulties we faced. They helped us to get in touch with the anger and the pain, but also with solutions. Seeing myself as an uninvolved, uncommunicative shell was devastating. Susan cried and cried for me as she saw my amazement, when I began to realize what I had become.

"One of the most important things I discovered was how our families affect us and our ways of thinking. I saw how my parents shaped and formed my life. I didn't know how to be an independent adult. I was a dependent husband and father, wanting Susan to take care of me and all my needs. I had allowed my parents to do all kinds of things for me because I was so afraid of failure that I didn't risk much of anything.

"I began to understand how this almost ruined our marriage. I had been prevented from seeing that I was capable of much more than they or I thought I could do.

"As each day passed, I felt both healing and doubt. How could we weave all this new understanding into our marriage and the way we related to each other?"

Susan picks up her part of the story. "Our pastor had sensed correctly that things were not right between Matt and me. Sometimes I felt like a spider hanging from a tiny filament of a web, but whenever our pastor called, I felt such love and hope. Although those phone calls didn't do much to make things different at our house, I felt strengthened and encouraged by his care and concern.

"It was during a particularly tumultuous week that Pastor Thompson urged us to go to Recovery of Hope. He assured us that we did not have to make any kind of commitment beyond the introductory session. Maybe we could find a little hope, he explained encouragingly.

"I couldn't imagine Matt consenting to go. I expected him to refuse because I thought he would see it as too threatening. When his reply was positive, I felt like a match had been lit and there was a tiny flicker of hope lighting my darkness.

"It wasn't easy making the decision to go for help. I was afraid of falling down, down, down, deeper into my dark hole. I cried a lot during that week as pain and buried anger bubbled up inside me. Several times I ran to the bathroom to physically throw up all the bad that I felt psychologically.

"I learned that Matt saw me, not as a woman, but as a mommy. I learned that, not unlike the Pharisees, I used God to make myself look better in 'church peoples' eyes.' I cried uncontrollably when Matt clung to me for comfort from his own personal pain.

"I saw my extended family as I never had before. They had not enhanced me as much as I thought. They had done many things well, but some things they did merely to exercise their parental authority and control. That authority had become so powerful over me that I now refused to let anyone gain that kind of control of me, not even God. In fact, I even found it hard to let anyone close to me have an opinion different from mine.

"My confusion with my parents' power led me to discredit Matt, to not trust his opinion, to ridicule him instead of support him. I was figuratively neutering Matt. He was nothing. I did not trust his judgments about anything. He was a role 'husband,' but I saw nothing worthwhile in him. If I had a financial question, I asked my father. If I had a sexual question or fear, I asked my mother. I didn't hesitate to discuss my 'neutered' husband or his disgusting nothingness.

"Confusing God with my biological father led me to create my own God, one who expected me to become a doer. The therapists pulled up the shades on my views of God and encouraged me to stand alone before God and to allow Matt to do the same.

"The healing that began that week was nothing short of miraculous. Matt began to see me beyond the mommy role and I began to see him as a unique and marvelous man. In the guest home where we stayed we had time to just be together, time without the children to talk, argue, pray and make love. Our relationship was reborn."

"During the following months," Matt continues, "we worked on those areas in our relationship that we had together identified as needy. We committed ourselves to more time together, to improving our efforts to accomplish household chores as a team. I decided to reduce my work hours. Reluctantly I approached my boss. He nodded his head, claimed he understood, and I began my first week of nine-hour days. Three weeks later I stood before him as he told me that I wasn't pulling my weight. How, he asked, was the work going to get done? Seeing that this was an impossible situation, I resigned my position as co-manager to take a job as a truck driver for the same company.

"It was hard at first to change from time at work to more time at home. I felt that I was out of my environment. I had many adjustments. The children loved my extra investment of time, and I became a new person in their eyes as well.

"I put my paper down and talked to Susan, and I discovered a friend. Sometimes the difference in the way we related frightened me. I didn't believe it could last. But slowly I began to trust this new relationship."

Susan speaks again. "Following our intensive week, I was extremely positive. I felt like I had been given the most wonderful gift, a new relationship! I was once again able to love Matt. I never believed it could be. But now I did believe in what happened with us and in the possibilities for the future.

"I clung to Matt. I clung too hard and depended too much on him. After all this work, I still suffered the headaches that my family doctor had diagnosed as psychological. I still felt failure. I felt dark and sometimes out of control.

"Matt tried to understand my emotional turmoil. He told me I puzzled him, but that he loved me. He encouraged me to call a competent psychologist. I hung up three times before I actually made the appointment. Inside of me there was box upon box of things I needed to work out, my feelings toward my mother and father and my hatred of myself.

"I wanted my moment in the sun, but I couldn't have that moment because I wasn't good enough for myself. The psychologist showed me the grace of God. He showed me how I was destroying myself with hatred and fear, and I grew.

"I am learning that my expectations are often not realistic for others or myself. I am learning to be satisfied and content with me as I am at this moment. I have found new freedom in discovering a God who does not demand but requests my response. Matt and I have scaled the wall that used to divide us. We share our time and our opinions with each other. Our relationship, which existed in a drought, no longer thirsts.

"Whenever we review this part of our lives, we experience some old familiar feelings. It is as though we put on our old glasses and see each other through those old lenses."

Susan concludes: "Matt used the newspaper to keep me away when we started to put our story on paper. I used the TV when Matt said, 'Let's get to it.' It seemed like a rerun of feelings and made us ask why we should go through this again. It all comes down to you," Susan looks up at the couples in difficulty who are listening to their story. "You and your marriage are worth the little discomfort we may feel in sharing our story with you. Hope is there for you, too. We wish you a clear path to find it."

3

For Better or For Worse

Russ was exhausted just thinking about what he would likely face when he got home at night. Would Amelia be in a good mood? Or would she have something to throw in his face again?

"Often we would drag on until two or three in the morning, with Amelia threatening suicide or running away from home. I was afraid of what she might do to herself when she was so completely out of control. *I* wasn't allowed to show *my* feelings. Someone had to be in control, and it was obvious it had to be me.

"Many times I dragged myself out of bed after only three or four hours of sleep and got ready for work while she slept in and even took a nap in the afternoon if she wanted. The bitterness inside me became almost unbearable when I thought of the unfairness of it all. Sometimes I found myself wishing I had let her go when she wanted to run away, or I hoped something would happen to her so I could get out of this mess and save face.

"It seemed like an impossible situation with no hope for change. I felt like a trapped animal with no way out. Yes, I had promised 'for better or for worse.' I had one consolation—it couldn't get much worse!" Russ grins ruefully.

Russ became concerned about the effect of all this turmoil on their sons. "What would people think if they knew the truth about our relationship? What would my parents think? After all, my dad had warned me about marrying Amelia. I could just hear him say, 'I told you, didn't I'" Russ continues. "It seemed like a no-win situation."

He considered running away himself. Maybe then she would

see what she was doing to him. Maybe then she would appreciate what he was doing for her and the boys. "But I couldn't bring myself to do that. My pride held me back. It would make me look better if people heard that she left. After all, it was the crazy one who always left," Russ remembers his internal reasoning.

Amelia jumps back in time as she tells of the events that led to their current situation. "At a very early age, I became fearful about relationships. I repeatedly told everyone that I would never marry. I would be a female hermit!

"But underneath my independent air I was an extremely lonely individual. I feared relationships, but I feared loneliness even more, and at the age of 24 I agreed to marry Russ.

"I had viewed sexual activity as the zenith of intimacy, the culmination of all that can possibly be shared. I had been lonely for so long I was more than ready for my fantasies to become realities. I believed we would spend most of our time in bed. Reality can be cruel and when the honeymoon was over, I was in for a rude awakening!

"Time and time again when Russ did not respond to my sexual advances, I began to panic. Where else was I going to find the kind of fulfillment I wanted, if not in our marriage? You just didn't run to someone else for sexual activity, although that thought became more of a plausible idea as our problems continued," Amelia says.

As she became increasingly desperate, Amelia decided to try one more approach. She bought a sexy negligee in hopes that it might "be the clue to solving the problem.

"As he lay in bed, I made my entrance into the room wearing my new lingerie. To my total dismay, he asked, 'How much did it cost?'" Amelia recalls with a tinge of hurt remaining. "I was devastated! I was so hurt and angry that I tore the thing off, threw it on the floor, and determined *never* to make a fool of myself like that again."

Amelia felt she had offered all she had, and had been rejected, again. The wall between them grew higher as she determined never again to let her sexual feelings and desire show. She, too, felt trapped.

"I could find no words to express all that was going on inside me. Feelings of being unloved, unwanted and undesirable hung over me like a big black cloud, a darkness so thick I could taste it," Amelia continues.

"I also saw him looking at other women and jealousy raged within me. I couldn't get him to look at *me* that way, yet he never missed an opportunity to scan someone else. When he looked at others I felt that my own physical appearance was under attack. He was looking at their bodies so I surmised that mine was inadequate. Even though he kept telling me it had nothing to do with *my* body, I kept shouting, 'Then why don't you look at me? You only look at thin, young, sexy women!"

Amelia began to feel more ugly, more unwanted, more used and "just plain old. I felt like a beggar waiting for a handout. I told myself there was no use in hoping for anything. After all, I must be repulsive to him."

Amelia had often heard her mother explain that it was the woman's responsibility to respond to the man, that a man just can't help himself when it comes to sex. Did that mean that women had no choice when they wanted intimacy? Why wasn't Russ attracted by her approaches, she wondered. What was wrong with her? She began believing that any woman could have him if she chose since he couldn't help himself. It was simply a matter of time since he was already looking. And her despair increased.

Russ felt Amelia wanted his total attention, that he was supposed to be "wrapped up" in her. "All the things I enjoyed doing had to go, unless we could do them together. Hunting, my favorite hobby, became a very sore spot. She couldn't understand why I could take off from work for that but I never took off work just to be with her. I began to fear that I would have to give up everything that didn't include her," Russ says.

"I became involved in committees and activities outside our home, and she continued to view them as competition. She felt she was losing. During those times that I sensed she was jealous and feeling rejected, I didn't know how to communicate to her that I loved her and wanted her. I truly wanted a deeper relationship with her, one where I would feel loved and trusted.

"I began looking at other women, seeing only what met the eye. I didn't really want someone else, but I didn't know how to tell her that. I thought that if she really loved me, she wouldn't treat me the way she did.

"She had an insatiable desire for my affection, my time and my attention. So I forced myself to do the things I thought a husband was supposed to do, but my heart wasn't in it. I felt inadequate in meeting her needs, and I couldn't understand why my desires and needs weren't the same as hers. My mom always seemed to get along with my dad without all this attention and fuss. Mom and Dad never showed affection for each other, at least that we saw. And we kids never got encouragement or affection, so what was the big deal?" Russ asked himself.

"Dad got to do the things he wanted to do that were fun, while Mom was at home with the kids. I thought it was because she loved him so much she wanted to make sure he had a good time. Why couldn't my wife want the same thing for me? Why couldn't she find something fun to do while I was gone?

"I was a do, do, do person. I worked in the store until late at night, then came to bed too tired to notice her. But at least I had a sense of accomplishment. She always talked about *being* what she wanted; I always came back with the question, 'Just tell me what I am supposed to *do*,'" Russ remembers.

"Russ and I came from very different backgrounds," Amelia continues. "In his world the men could do anything they wanted without considering how their wives might feel. I abhorred the way I saw them treat women.

"Russ wanted to go deer hunting. I was heartbroken. I thought we were in this marriage together and here I was, nine months pregnant with our first child, and he didn't even consider the possibility of my having the baby alone while he was off having fun somewhere.

"We fought! And he stayed home but I knew it was not because he cared. He had given in in order to keep peace."

Hunting continued to be an issue. Russ's dad had always gone; why shouldn't he? Women were supposed to be submissive and consider the wishes of their husbands.

"Russ would cross his arms in front of himself and give me

one of those 'Here we go again' looks. That stance and his silent response made me feel as though the judge had already determined the case and it was closed.

"The more hurt and angry I was, the more indifferent he became. I began to believe that I was not only a loser, but that I was crazy as well.

"I could have handled anger and hate better than his indifference. I wished and even prayed that I could treat him with the same indifference, but I couldn't," Amelia says.

Amelia lived with a host of unanswered questions. Was she really that different from others? Why did God make her this way? Why didn't he do anything to help? Was this all there was to life? Amelia's ups and downs seemed closely timed into the 28 day cycle she went through month after month. One diagnosis pointed to severe PMS, pre-menstrual syndrome. She tried special diets, exercises, stress reduction techniques, vitamins, antidepressants, hormones, counseling and more counseling. But she continued to be depressed. "I was depressed because I was always depressed!" she recalls with wry humor.

"The rage and hostility I battled with were the most embarrassing part of all," Amelia says. "I knew I was supposed to be kind, to love and on and on, blah, blah, blah, all I had been taught from little on up. But no matter what I did I could not control the horrendous feelings I had. Sometimes I would attack Russ physically, hating him for not loving me. And I hated myself for my criminal behavior. I just wanted to run.

"Sometimes I panicked, thinking that I must live like this the rest of my life. Everyone would have been happier if I had just disappeared. I cursed the fact that my only sister had died in childbirth and I had lived. Why couldn't it have been me?

"The agony I was experiencing with Russ brought back painful memories of my childhood. I grew up in a remote part of New Mexico. My happiest memories were always those times that I spent alone.

"I had one brother, a year younger than I, who was, for reasons I did not understand, my mother's idol. Knowing that cut me like a knife.

"In her way, my mother loved me, but it came through as

simply her duty. My brother could do nothing wrong. I was *always* the troublemaker. He had a violent temper, but I would be accused of doing something to set him off.

"Mother let me know that she disliked her mother-in-law and saw that person in me. Being the object of her hostility created an obsession within me. I wanted to be loved because of who I was.

"I thought somewhere, someone would surely want me because I was me, female. I hoped our marriage would bring me the one thing I wanted more than anything else in life—to be loved and accepted just for being me.

"But now I felt tricked! I had married rejection personified and my dream world was fast becoming a nightmare. If I died, would God even want me? I no longer had the energy to fight. I didn't care what happened next."

Russ remembers "Amelia hounding me that I should understand her feelings. Once in a while I responded in the way she wanted and she would thank me for caring. But that was equally as baffling. I would think, that can't be the answer; that's too simple!

"Everytime Amelia tried some new medication or treatment, I hoped we were on the right track, but it was always short-lived and we were soon back where we had started. Fear and disappointment returned, covering up the hope we had. It was like living on a seesaw. The downs came more often than the ups, but there was a flicker of hope now and then. I came to believe that if we could just hold out long enough, we would hit on the right combination.

"As I sat in a group one day," recalls Amelia, "I noticed that each of us was reacting differently because of our past programming. In that moment I saw in part why I was so angry with Russ: I did not understand him. I determined to learn *who* this person was I had married. Never mind if he didn't understand me; I was going to make an all out effort to find out who he was!"

Amelia prayed for strength in her weakness, health for her illness and guidance for her journey. She believes God answered in a rather unexpected way.

"One of the pieces that first fell into place for us was being able to talk about the pain I felt when Russ looked at and fantasized about other women. My greatest need was to have him appreciate my body. He told me he imagined that the women he looked at were affirming him and appreciating his many accomplishments. I had vaguely heard him say something to that effect before. In fact, he often talked about how I never gave him credit for the things he did. But I had not really heard him because I did not have that same need to be credited for the tasks I performed. Now I began to glimpse why he wanted to hunt, ride motorcycle, work on church committees and even fantasize. He was looking for basic fulfillment too, and he was not getting it from me. We had begun, but the work wasn't over!"

Russ remembers learning to understand each other's needs and feelings little by little. "Once in a counseling session we were asked to talk about a situation that happened in our lives, as the counselor observed. He stopped me after a particular response I made to Amelia and said, 'I sense anger in your reply. Are you angry at your wife?' I denied that I was, but he insisted that he detected anger in my voice. I suddenly realized that, yes, I was angry. Angry for all the time we wasted in fighting. Angry about all the things I had wanted to do and gave up just to keep peace. Angry at the sleepless nights. Angry at her beating on me, and on and on. It was a big step. For the first time I was able to acknowledge my feelings, express them and ask forgiveness.

"Soon another barrier was broken down. We went to a Marriage Encounter weekend where we were asked to communicate on a feeling level. I had been programmed from little on up not to show my feelings, but now I was able to see how readily Amelia responded when I expressed how I felt. In fact, she was open to my doing things I enjoyed, as long as we talked about it first, she was included in the planning and believed I understood her feelings."

There was still the matter of the PMS. Despite many efforts to find solutions, the symptoms continued: rage, intense emotional pain, feelings of being out of control, depression and hopelessness. "I struggled with living on the edge of insanity," Amelia remembers painfully. "It hung over me like death itself. I knew I simply could not continue to live like this."

Meanwhile Amelia continued to function productively, reaching out to people, finding ways to be creative and helpful. She decided to take a Clinical Pastoral Education course to keep her occupied and feeling good about herself during the winter months.

"I became part of a team working with patients who had experienced much abuse in their past. While I was deeply troubled by what I heard, at the same time I was amazed at the progress they were making in putting their lives back together.

"One of the psychiatrists particularly impressed me. I remember thinking one day that if he could help people with such dysfunctional backgrounds, maybe he could help me. My background wasn't nearly as ugly as most of these people's."

In August Amelia made her first appointment and began to meet with the psychiatrist on a weekly basis. She read that women who suffer with PMS often come from highly dysfunctional families. This was different from what she had known earlier, that it was basically a biological problem. Another source said that most women who have had sexual abuse in their childhoods struggle with intense PMS symptoms.

"I thought that element wasn't applicable to me because I had not been sexually abused as a child. But maybe my past had been more difficult than I knew.

"We began to explore my childhood carefully. When the psychiatrist asked me about various issues, I knew simply that something was creating a very BIG problem for me, but, no, I was not sexually abused as a child."

Amelia began to recall several women she had met who had blocked all memories of their past sexual abuse. But she continued to believe that she would have remembered something as traumatic as that, had it happened to her. She knew her home wasn't "normal," but it certainly wasn't that abnormal.

"One day," Amelia recounts, "I was sitting in my favorite chair at home, pondering all these things, when I found myself saying aloud, 'Could my PMS and rage possibly come from some hidden agenda.....such as sexual abuse?' I could hardly think it, let alone ask it. I took a deep breath and said, 'Lord, hold my hand, because if it's true, I want to know. I want the truth, no matter what I have to face. I am sick of struggling and feeling defeated.'

"The unbelievable began to happen. As I continued to work with my therapist, dreams, flashbacks, sensations and memories slowly filtered from my subconscious to my conscious. Pictures I had long forgotten began to accompany the feelings that had hounded me for as long as I could remember. A picture of a bedroom, complete with details and sensations. I passed it off as imagination. Why would I remember something so ridiculous, I asked the doctor.

"My mother would have known this particular room and I had to find out if I was imagining it or not. After a couple days I found the courage to call her. By asking leading questions I was able to get her to describe this room to me. To my great dismay, she described it exactly as I was remembering it. But how could this be? How could I ever trust my mind to tell me the truth after all these years? I had been only two years old. Yet I *had* remembered precisely.

"I felt I was thrown into a dark hole that fell deep into the center of the earth. Even though Russ and I had begun to make some progress, I saw no way out of this mess. What had I gotten myself into? Wouldn't it have been better not to know?

"But the more I allowed the feelings, sensations, dreams and memories to penetrate my conscious thought, the more I realized that this indeed must be the mystery that had kept me bound all these years. The rage I felt emerging now was so incredibly fierce that I feared I would be swallowed completely. I trusted no one. Darkness and doubt hung like shadows in every corner, waiting to wrap their spidery webs around my mind. Day and night God reminded me that he had me by the hand. Russ was there beside me, encouraging me in the best way he knew."

Little by little, the mystery was unfolding. Amelia continues softly, her voice fragile, "My abusers had used fairy tales to weave the threads of sexual abuse. Make-believe and reality had been deliberately mixed together so that I had been forced to believe that my mind was incapable of telling me the truth about anything.

"I had been introduced, at age two, to the experience of living on the edge of insanity. The result has truly been a living nightmare. But now for the first time in my life a lot of things are beginning to make sense.

"Even though these past several months have been hard, what I've learned has been worth it. My past is still not completely resolved. The feelings have not all been washed away. But I am in process. I am freer from pain, and I have hope. God used some fine people to help me find that toddler locked inside my body, made captive and hurt by those who were not themselves free. Today I still hate them, but, eventually, because of God's great love for me, I will be able to release them and no longer be bound by them.

"In our marriage the shadows are disappearing. Hope is shining in places where it hasn't shone before. Our marriage is not a mistake. It just needed a lot of help," Amelia concludes.

Russ adds, "It isn't always easy; in fact, it's very hard work sometimes. But we find that being transparent with each other significantly lowers the walls we had built. I want to understand Amelia's pain, and, even though I can't know what it's really like to have experienced all she has, I do know that the better I know her, the more I love her!"

Amelia and Russ often pass along this blessing to couples who hear their story: "May the shadows that shroud your journey in life be dispelled by the recovery of hope."

4

Can We Ever Be The Same Again?

"I was unbelievably rude to Betty. And I did it deliberately. I figured if I could force her to initiate a divorce, I would look like the injured one, and my family and friends would support me. I felt a little sorry for her when I saw her suffering, but I was stubborn enough to want to continue with my new life, no matter what it did to her."

Howard recalled the events that led him and Betty to doubt that their marriage could be reconciled. Betty's eyes still showed a hint of the hurt she experienced.

✦

"Hey, look at that blonde damsel in distress over there," Howard whistled as he stood in line to board the plane. Betty was just ahead of him and his buddies. They were all students at the University, all in a holiday mood as they headed home for Christmas. Betty was tearful and terrified of flying. Howard broke out of the line, went to her with his handkerchief in hand, touched her shoulder, wiped her tears and told her that everything would be alright.

"Look out, Howard!" his friend said prophetically.

That was Christmas break of their freshman year. Howard and Betty said no more than hello until a spring outing when they both took an afternoon off from studying for exams down by the lake. The dock was crowded; spirits ran high. Several of

Howard's fraternity brothers playfully picked Betty up and threw her off the dock. She landed flat on her back, tried to catch her breath, then climbed out of the water in tears.

"I ran down to where she was, tried to help dry her off, asked her if she was okay, kissed her on the forehead and told her everything was all right. I thought, *deja vu*. We talked for a while, fed the swans, chased the ducks and then walked back to the dorm in the rain. She said thank you, we kissed, and that's how it all began. I was convinced that this lady was someone really special and everything would be wonderful," Howard recalls.

Howard and Betty saw themselves as two mature, well educated and talented individuals when they got married. The first years of their marriage were filled with hope and high expectations of themselves and each other. Then Howard began to have some difficulties in graduate school and in locating a job. His sense of competence and confidence began to fade, and his hopes for a career became less certain. "I was caught in a vicious circle," Howard says. "The more depressed I grew, the less hope I had and the less effort I put into anything I did. I felt as if I were slowly sinking, as if all the bright lights of my life were burning out. For two years I spun my wheels, all the while sensing, although not really showing it on the outside, decay occurring in our marriage.

"Betty seemed successful in everything she tried. Her career was moving right along according to plan and she had lots of friends. I began to feel as though we were moving in two different directions: Betty up, Howard down. This became even more pointed when we were with her success-oriented family."

Howard remembers a visit to Betty's home one summer when he was feeling especially vulnerable. Everyone was on the patio enjoying an evening of laughing, talking, teasing chatter.

"Well Howard, how's the career coming? Found a job yet?" queried Betty's research physicist brother, Bob. He had just finished telling them about the large grant he had received for continuing his research project. There was no place for Howard to hide. He tried joking about "living by the sweat of my frau" but it didn't work. He could detect Betty's frustration—or was it embarrassment—growing. His feelings of loneliness and separation were taking on a paranoid sense of discomfort. He began to actually believe that he was inadequate and incompetent in most areas of his life, especially with Betty's family.

"My frustration turned into bitterness and anger that burned deeper and hotter every day," says Howard. "It seemed as though Betty was going on her merry way, and the only time she was concerned about me was when she would ask, 'What did you do today?' meaning what did I do that was productive—like finding a job. Never mind that I did the food shopping or the cleaning, or cooking and washing dishes. Those seemed important only when Betty did them. I began to see her every question and comment as a personal attack. Even when she complimented me I thought she was insincere and patronizing."

One late summer day Betty announced to Howard that she was going to graduate school in Eugene, and that she would be living away from him during that time. All his despair increased "several orders in magnitude" until he lost hope for anything good in his life. But after a few weeks of deep despair, Howard recalls, "A new sense of angry resolve arose in me and I was more determined than ever to make my life successful."

✦

Every story has two sides. Each player tends to recall events differently. Betty remembers feeling full of hope and confidence. "We had four wonderful years in college together when we were inseparable. I was excited about our marriage; I knew our love was special and would last forever. I expected those great years in college to be continually replayed in our marriage. I was living in a fantasy world. We were never very good at facing reality in my family.

"We began our married lives in Seattle where I had been teaching. Howard got a job tutoring at the same school and after a year began working at a department store. I knew that was just temporary because I had bigger plans for us!

"The two years in Seattle flew by and then we made a move to Portland so Howard could attend graduate school. I would support us, something which I had always heard was a romantic thing to do. I worked at a restaurant and Howard began classes. Then I got my first teaching job! It was a tough one, but I knew the situation was only temporary.

"All I did was work, teaching during the day and waitressing at night. My fantasy world disappeared in a hurry. Our plans seemed to be falling apart. The one and a half years in Portland stretched to two, then three, then four and five and Howard still didn't have his degree. I couldn't figure out his lack of motivation. Our family didn't do things this way. So in my frustration I worked harder and stayed away from home as much as possible.

"As my anger built I decided that at least I would do something about *my* life. That's when I made up my mind to go to graduate school for a Master's in special education. I wasn't going to lose my identity and goals just because Howard couldn't get his act together.

"Howard came home one evening with a bouquet of flowers, and I knew he had gotten a job," Betty recalls.

"Guess what," Howard had called, holding the bouquet behind him with a boyish grin on his face. "I snagged that job at the research center that I really wanted. So I'll not only have a good income, I'll also be in line for becoming part of the research team. We'll write and publish, and you can go to school here and won't have to move to Eugene and...," on he rattled excitedly, handing Betty the flowers and kissing her on her forehead. Everything would be all right again.

But Betty wasn't impressed. She decided to continue with her plans for school and promptly moved to Eugene. There was no discussion, no negotiating.

"I remember well the day Howard left me off at the home of an elderly, retired professor where I would stay during the week (I planned to go home weekends). We stood outside that house and cried. I knew what I was doing was wrong, but I was determined to go through with my plans. Howard was there with his handkerchief, trying again to make things all right, but he couldn't."

"The day I dropped Betty off at Eugene was the most painful

day I ever experienced. But I didn't think I could let her know. I didn't want her to know how scared I was to have the person who had been the focal point of my life, even if some of our times had been bad, to be so suddenly removed. I really thought she might change her mind about leaving for school since I had landed such a great job. It was the kind of job that even Betty's parents would have enjoyed bragging about.

"I felt empty and lost as I drove home alone along the Willamette River. It was as though someone had pulled my heart out. Maybe, I thought, this pain isn't all bad. It must mean there's still something left of our marriage. At least I feel something. But I was unable to get my focus off my own struggles. I was going to make the most of my new job.

"'Good work' my first evaluation at the lab said. 'You show great ability and promise. We're glad to have you on board as part of the team. We want to encourage you to do postgraduate studies at UCLA. The success of your most recent project and the articles you published indicate to us that you are a fine researcher.' My ego swelled and I started to savor hope. Recognition by my peers and supervisors fed my fires and I began to see a new brightly lighted picture of my future, in stark contrast to the dark, hopeless years in my recent past. That dark past included my marriage and Betty; my bright future did not, but it did include someone else.

"Hi, honey, I'm here!" Betty called cheerfully arriving home one weekend. She had actually looked forward to seeing Howard and made a beeline to his parents' home where Howard was living. But she was met, to her surprise, with a less than enthusiastic response. "Then one awful day," Betty recalls, "Howard told me he was no longer in love with me and that he didn't think we were going to make it as husband and wife. I had thought, even though he seemed distant at times, that things were beginning to come together for us. I couldn't believe he was giving up on our commitment to each other.

"He told me he was staying at the lab late to work. But some of his explanations made no sense at all. He would say one thing one moment and totally contradict himself the next. I was becoming confused and nervous. I lost 20 pounds and felt like

I was losing control of myself. This was not the man I married, but I couldn't figure out what was going on. Howard's personality seemed to be changing before my eyes. I knew that I needed help," Betty concluded.

The "someone else" Howard met at the lab was both friendly and understanding. She was rebounding from a divorce, and they found they had a lot in common and could talk without effort. They gave each other a lot of time and attention and soon began to feel they genuinely cared about each other.

"I knew what was happening, but was powerless, by my own choice, to stop it. Deep inside I knew it was wrong but it felt too good, especially after all the hurt and loneliness I had experienced with Betty. The feelings I was beginning to have were positive, hopeful, wonderful," Howard remembers.

"The once benign insignificant problems in our marriage had spread into a raging cancer, bent on destroying our marriage. As the guilt inside me began to grow, death was no longer just a metaphor for me, but a real physical possibility I found nearly preferable to life.

"I couldn't just tell Betty I was having an affair, even though I thought the signs were pretty obvious if she cared to notice. So I finally told her I didn't love her anymore. What I really meant was that I had no *feelings* of love, and that I wanted a divorce. That's when I began the rudeness campaign."

About that time Betty's younger sister Audrey found out she had leukemia. The entire family was stunned. Betty left immediately for Edmonton to be with Audrey and the family. The few days turned into weeks.

"Howard, I'm staying just a little longer because my family really needs me," Betty would say each time she called him.

"How in the world could I tell her how much I needed her too?" Howard asked. "One night at 11:00 p.m. her words cut so deeply that I ran from the house and kept running until I vomited and nearly passed out from exhaustion, but the problem remained. Time after time, it seemed to me, Betty's family spoke and we listened. They called; we jumped. But when conflicts surfaced between us, we quickly put the lid on so as not to rock the boat."

Slowly, but surely, their lines of communication were shutting down. "I reached a point where I figured, why bother?" Howard says. "I didn't know how to communicate my loneliness and hopelessness. We had been married before God and we both had the same beliefs and values. But the very principles on which we had built our lives and our marriage were crumbling, and the foundation of our marriage no longer seemed to exist. I had a great deal of religious head knowledge, but it had little effect on my life and our marriage. Besides, I found it easier and more convenient to fit God into my plans, rather than paying attention to the operating instructions laid out by the Designer.

"And for awhile it looked as though things were going to happen according to my plan. Betty would see that I didn't love her anymore and that I wanted out of the marriage. But rather suddenly there was a different Betty—calm, peaceful and firm in her commitment to the marriage. At first I was angry. She was going to foul up my entire scheme, so I decided to call up the heavy artillery. I would tell her I was having an affair. That should do it."

But the strangest thing happened when he confessed to her what he had done. "She forgave me!" Howard says, surprise still apparent on his face. "Our emotions exploded into a river of tears—Betty's from pain and love, mine from pain and confusion. I was really more confused than ever."

Howard, desperate for someone to talk to, found himself at a friend's home. After several glasses of scotch and some conversation that wasn't particularly helpful, Howard drove home, north in the southbound lane. He wondered aloud if he was trying to commit suicide. The experience absolutely frightened him. But the following weeks brought him greater confusion and guilt. He was sure he didn't love Betty and that he did love someone else.

Betty recalls her experience at that time. "When our marriage started falling apart and Howard talked about divorce, I panicked. We loved each other too much!" But then it was as if someone was lifting a curtain from my eyes, allowing me to see all the mistakes I had made. It was terribly painful but also helpful. I realized that I often thought of myself first and the things *I* wanted to accomplish. Howard was in such despair over not finding work, but I only got upset with him, instead of understanding and supporting him. In my anger and resentment, I retaliated by taking off for graduate school at a time when he needed me most, giving a pretty clear signal that I cared more about my life than his or ours."

Betty became aware that Howard often felt threatened by her family and the closeness she shared with them. When she couldn't find a way to change his feelings, she took even more opportunities to be with them, although it added strain to their marriage.

Another major problem became clear to her at this time. "When we were married, we not only committed our lives to each other but to God. But as time went by, we neglected the spiritual part of our marriage. I remember pleading with Howard that we try to work at this again together, but he only laughed and said it was too late. That was so uncharacteristic of him because he had always been deeply interested in spiritual matters."

The fact of her own selfishness kept coming to Betty as she thought about their marriage. "I remembered a time when I planned a trip to Canada with a friend of mine from work. Just before she and I were to leave, Howard came down with pleurisy. He was quite sick, but I wasn't about to change my plans. As I left, his mother walked in the door with a prescription she had gotten for him. I was too blind to see what I was doing to us.

"Another time, I took a trip to Phoenix with my younger sister. My Dad had asked us to accompany him to Arizona for a national golf tournament. Then I decided to invite a guy from Virginia, a friend of our family's whom I knew enjoyed golf. I thought it was all very innocent, and I viewed it as a chance to spend some time with my younger sister whom I seldom saw. Little did I realize what a devastating effect my simplistic way of thinking would have on Howard and me.

"I assumed Howard and his love would always be there, waiting, that I could go on pursuing what I wanted to do and he would always understand and support me. And I didn't see my part in it."

Armed with new insight, Betty told Howard how wrong she had been, how much she wanted to change things if he would just give her a chance. When he didn't welcome her new understanding, she began to wonder if there was something more going on inside him that she couldn't put her finger on. Something didn't make sense. Howard was coming to some conclusions of his own. One day, alone in the woods, he was able to sort out three realities: that he needed help to get out of this situation, that he really did want to do what was right, and that he had deeply hurt someone to whom he had committed has life. "Worst of all, I had willfully turned my back on all that I had believed was holy and good. Could I be forgiven? Whatever happened, I knew that the course out of this deep, dark pit would be long and painful, full of a great deal of work and effort.

"Betty convinced me to go with her to see our pastor. I didn't like him or what he had to say because he challenged me. But he did have some new light for what seemed like a hopeless situation.

"He persuaded me to hang onto any thread of faith I had left so I could decide to do what I knew to be right, one step at a time. I felt very much like a young boy trying to ask a girl for his first dance—nervous, weak, embarrassed, incapable and scared to death."

Betty recalls her despair and helplessness during this time of uncertainty. It was affecting her health. She was still losing weight and slept very little. "At one particularly low point I found myself walking about a mile from home at three o'clock in the morning in the middle of January. I didn't have shoes, gloves or anything on that would protect me from the weather. Somehow I made my way back home and spent the rest of the night rocking back and forth in a chair, still unable to sleep and to stop the trembling. The next morning I went for help."

There was still more hurt to come. It was the missing piece about Howard's behavior. "I vividly recall the day Howard confessed to me that he had been having an affair. But in that moment I felt a calmness come over me that I never experienced before. *Now* I understood all the inconsistent and inconsiderate behavior, all the lies, all the ugliness and rudeness, all the late nights at the lab. The puzzle piece fit perfectly. What amazed me was that I could sit there and still love this man more than ever before, even though it was the most painful thing I had ever gone through," Betty says.

But there was more. Although Howard had finally opened himself to Betty, he still wasn't sure if the marriage could work. He seemed unable to let go of the guilt he was carrying, even though his confession seemed to lift a great burden from him.

Howard explains, "I was learning the great healing power of unconditional love; I was experiencing it from Betty. When I could confess what I had done and was truly sorry, her love began to heal my deep ugly wounds immediately. That love from my wife and from God began to fill me with the warmest and fullest sense of joy and hope I had ever known.

"I had totally violated a trust that Betty had placed in me. And it was going to take time to rebuild her trust and her belief that I loved her and desired *her*—not someone else. Each morning I left to go to work I saw the conflict in Betty's eyes, but each night when I came home I could see her joy. We were rebuilding, one day at a time."

Howard and Betty began attending church together, and for the first time met other couples who cared enough to encourage them and to hold them accountable for their relationship.

"I felt like I was conditioning for athletic competition," Howard grins. "Every exercise, every drill was working me into better and better shape. New life was being breathed into our marriage which had atrophied to the point of death."

Much of that new life came from practicing little things that nurture any relationship—a love note in a briefcase or hunting coat, flowers for no special reason, a phone call from work.

Howard uses the metaphor of a large solid bone like the femur, the large thigh bone. "That bone—our marriage—received a tremendous blow resulting in a painful break. The break had to be reset and given time to heal, with the right kind of careful and constant care. The pain is lessening as the bone grows stronger. It is finally healing and is sturdier than ever before."

"After Howard's confession to me," Betty continues, "and the realization that we had both been forgiven, our lives began to change, rapidly at first because we were working so hard at it, but then more slowly and steadily. We were rediscovering each other and learning things about each other that we hadn't known. Sometimes it has been very hard work, but I can hardly believe the entirely new view of marriage I have. Howard changed before my eyes. He has become more loving, more considerate, concerned about meeting my needs. And I am discovering what a pleasure it is to have my husband first in my heart and thoughts, not myself."

Howard and Betty acknowledge that their emotions ran strong early on in their reconciling process. But the hard work ahead of them could not be fueled alone by euphoria and hope. They sought counseling. They became actively involved in church where they had constant contact with new friends who held the same beliefs they did, who were also committed to making their marriages strong and healthy. "We realize now how isolated we had become and how important encouragement and support from friends really is."

The two of them began to enjoy each other's company more and started doing things together just for fun: fishing trips in the Pacific, saving for a trip to Mexico and realizing that goal, getting up on a Saturday morning and going out for breakfast. "Washing dishes can even be fun when we do it together!" Howard chuckles.

"I love when Howard asks me for a date," Betty admits. "We've come to realize that we cannot take each other for granted. And I've learned how important it is to accept Howard the way he is without trying to change him."

Betty and Howard acknowledge their ongoing hard times, in spite of the new commitment they made to each other and their marriage. "I still struggle periodically with doubt and lack of trust in Howard. Distrust rears its ugly head at the most unsuspecting times and then I feel insecure again. But I can talk about it with Howard and that makes all the difference," Betty says. "We continue to work on the relationship with my family. Howard still contends with that issue at times."

"It's not a new battle," Howard continues. "I felt they saw themselves as socially, economically and intellectually better than I. So it makes sense that Betty looked to them instead of me for advice and help, that she tried to meet their needs and expectations first, letting mine or ours fall into line later. So we each have areas that need time, love and constant attention.

"We've learned to set our time together as a priority. It's easy to let it slip by, but at least we are aware of those dangers and really work hard at spending time with each other."

Howard and Betty report that their journey as husband and wife is full of hope and promise and hard work! They are both grateful that they chose to stay with each other on the journey, and that "God has given us another chance." Can things ever be the same again? Yes and no. But forgiveness is a miracle maker; it can cause to be what logically has no right to be—reconciliation, hope and restoration.

5

Systems And Themes: Independence-Dependence

The concept of "family systems" is one way of understanding people and their behavior. Simply put, it suggests that persons can be best understood if they are seen as part of the connections and relationships which surround them. In more familiar words, "the whole is greater than the sum of its parts," and, further, each part can be understood only in the context of the whole.

What does this have to do with marriages? In the case of couples experiencing difficulty, it may mean that something happened within "the system" to tip the relationship off balance. What may have once worked for a family or couple, for a variety of reasons isn't working anymore. This disruption may come from outside the couple, such as the loss of a job or a crop failure that causes financial pressures, from the death of a parent or child, from a debilitating illness, or some normal life cycle occurrences such as a child leaving for college. The point is, as one part is affected or changed, every other part in the system is affected.

There is yet another kind of system that affects marriages— those distinctive beliefs and patterns that families (systems) have, which each spouse brings into the marital relationship. These patterns affect how each spouse handles whatever happens. One may come from a family where the message has been to "Grin and bear it," or "You can't be sick, we have work to do!" The other may have heard, "Don't over–do it, you'll make yourself sick." One may make decisions based on "What will people think?" The other "doesn't care what people think; this is our decision." These two persons experience and deal with decision-making, a crisis or change very differently.

Most couples do not or cannot have an awareness of these differences during courtship. They negotiate or dance around some matters that they subconsciously sense are too controversial to deal with. They find a way of relating on these issues, usually without talking directly about them even in the early part of their relationship. Behaviors eventually become organized around these "themes." A theme is a specific emotional issue around which a couple or family may have numerous disagreements or conflict (Papp: 14).

All of us come from families with many of these themes; usually we have not identified them, although we may know subconsciously our role in them. In a marriage they may develop something like this:

•One person is very responsible; the other rather irresponsible.

•One person acts as teacher; the other as a learner or student.

•One person wants to be very close; the other does things to maintain distance.

•One person has a position of authority; the other acts helpless or maintains feelings of helplessness.

These positions, of course, may shift in different situations, but the general theme is often predictable and stays the same (Papp: 14).

Couples frequently describe themselves in relation to each other in these ways, clearly believing that they really are that way!

"I knew he felt lonely and unimportant, but I thought if I just loved him enough he would feel good about himself and everything would be okay." She thinks that if she is just a "good enough" wife, she can not only make him feel good, but she will also feel as though she has accomplished her task.

Her husband may then say, "My wife is just a stronger person than I am. There are a lot of people who depend on her, including me." He thus acknowledges his weaknesses and his need for his wife to take care of him and make decisions for him so that he doesn't have to. And then, if the decisions turn out to be poor ones, he can blame her!

Most often couples choose each other with great accuracy and perform functions for each other, meeting each other's needs in a complementary way. But there often comes a time when this kind of give-and-take gets thrown off balance. She begins to weary of the "hidden contract" she is to carry out, of always caring for him and making sure he isn't lonely or feeling unimportant. She may begin to feel trapped or smothered because of his increasing dependence on her. He, on the other hand, may begin to see her as domineering, making his decisions for him, and resents her "taking care of" him or rescuing him. One spouse described her experience with an independent–dependent theme as the "vine that was slowly choking its support system." Another pictured his as a "fly, trapped in a huge spider web, each hurt being one strand of the web." This kind of restlessness agitates the rest of the system, often involving the children in these interactions.

Thus the themes begin to change when each grows dissatisfied with the way the give–and–take is being negotiated. These central themes can become the focus of some highly charged interactions. When the arrangement of teacher–learner or pursuer–distancer (or whatever the theme may be) becomes intolerable enough, one partner will act to change those roles, while the other partner will act to maintain the familiar.

Although change is unsettling and may temporarily unbalance the relationship, risking new behaviors and ways of relating, and creating new themes, can be the key to mutually satisfying partnership.

Independence – Dependence

"The event was small," Amy says, remembering a time before Christmas several years ago, "but with everything else I was going through, it was the last straw. I felt overwhelmed and was ready to end our marriage."

It was Sunday afternoon and time to put up the Christmas tree. Living in New England, the family had a long tradition of making a trip to a neighbor's farm, cutting the tree and, with great ceremony and anticipation, putting it up in the living room. The boys were all excited and began to unpack the Christmas ornaments. But as all of us know, those "happy family times" can sometimes be anything but happy.

"We looked forward to this event for several weeks and found a lovely tree. Jay had been having trouble with his back so it was difficult for him to help much with the actual cutting of the tree. I understood that, and the boys and I made a great show of sawing it down!

"But when we got back to the house, it seemed he wanted to give directions about where and how the tree should be set up. Of course he couldn't help because of his back. He was getting pretty good at that—demanding that he be taken care of but wanting to give orders as to how things should be done. I wondered sometimes how bad his back really was," confesses Amy.

"We're going to put the tree in the corner," Jay announced from his reclining position on the couch.

"No, Dad," their son Mike responded. "We want it so all the neighbors can see it, too!"

"I agree with Mike," Amy said. "If we put it in the corner we will have to move a lot of furniture," which of course Jay couldn't help do. But he was determined not to have the tree "blocking the window" and proceeded to give directions about how the furniture should be moved and rearranged.

"But Dad," pleaded Jason, their other son, "that would look dumb!"

"Nobody in this family seems to like any of my ideas," Jay said petulantly. "And nobody cares if my back hurts."

"That was really hard to swallow," recalls Amy. But falling into the familiar pattern of caretaking, she finally told him if his back hurt so much, he should go to bed. "But *I* was tired of feeling like his mother, and *he* resented being told what to do. I felt trapped. It was like Scrooge was determined to ruin our holiday event."

Amy recognizes that as the oldest in a family of six children, she was most at home in the role of caretaking, believing that somehow she was responsible to keep things together and make everyone happy.

"But I was angry. Our family time was ruined—again. Jay was an adult man. I felt I needed to build a wall around the boys to protect them from his insensitivity. And I was trying so hard to be the perfect wife. I kept getting messages from Jay like, 'What's wrong with these potatoes?' 'Why don't you get the boys to help around the house?' 'I wish you would want to make love more often.'

"I felt like a little girl again, struggling to make a perfect A, but I just couldn't succeed. I asked myself whether I could ever be a good enough wife for him? The confusion and frustration I felt was that I was not his mother, nor was I a little girl. I was his wife!"

Jay's part of the story must also be understood. "I grew up with a learning disability. Academics were bad enough, but my disability also affected my coordination. I hated to play baseball. I often struck out and nobody wanted me on their team. I remember how lonely I felt waiting, always the last to be chosen. When I asked Amy to marry me and she said yes, I was so happy. I had been chosen! I wasn't on the outside looking in anymore!"

"The problem was that Jay needed me too much," Amy adds. "When we married I knew I would have to do certain things because of his dyslexia. But it got to the place that he was so dependent on me, he counted on me to do all his thinking as well, which he was perfectly capable of doing himself.

"I was strangling," she says, "like a tree with a vine winding itself around the trunk for support. And when the tree grew, as I felt I was growing, the tension increased and the vine slowly choked its support system. I was being choked by a relationship with Jay and I felt like I was dying."

"I couldn't understand why Amy was telling me she felt like a mother to me," Jay recalls. "I had a great job, I was a good provider—wasn't that enough? It wasn't as though she had to take care of me. Her attitude affected everything, from decision-making to love-making and the roles we took. She said she couldn't enjoy making love when she felt like my mother!" Jay recalls. "That became the focus of a lot of our problems. Sometimes I wondered if she really loved me anymore."

With the help of a counselor Amy began to realize that her need to fix things often led to Jay's dependence on her. "When he had a problem I was somehow sure that it was my fault and that I should do something to remedy the situation. I began to realize that I was responsible for myself, and he was responsible for handling his own problems. That lifted a big burden from my shoulders."

Jay began to see that he was a competent person, able to think for himself and make good decisions. If a choice he made didn't work, it was his responsibility and not Amy's. "I learned that I often set myself up to fail and then blamed others. That's changing," Jay says with a smile. "We began to have more realistic expectations of each other as well. I've picked up some hobbies again; I'm getting a lot of satisfaction out of wood–carving. One of my carvings won a purple ribbon at the county fair recently," Jay says with modest enthusiasm.

"The other thing I discovered," Amy explains with satisfaction, "is that I was so caught up in the need to care for others that I had no dreams for myself. Now I find myself planning things I want to do and then making them happen. I've written some music to use at church, something I used to only dream about, and now it's becoming a reality. I've even had some of my music arrangements published."

Recently Amy wrote Jay a letter that included this paragraph, "My hope is that we will become two strong people, able to travel down our own streets and celebrate our uniqueness, then come together to celebrate our unity. That kind of relationship gives me the freedom I need so that I can respond to your love and love you in return."

6

Give The Tree Time To Grow

Bob still laughs about their first encounter. "I had this little old black car with holes in the floor and we had to dodge the mud puddles so we wouldn't get soaked. But we had a lot of fun!"

"He wore cowboy boots so he didn't mind getting wet like I did," Becky adds fondly. "I sat with my legs curled under me to keep dry! I thought it was a real coup when I finally got him out of those boots and flannel shirts and wide belts with big buckles. I used to ask him if he thought our little boys would run around someday with cowboy boots wearing huge belts with big buckles that said 'DAD' on them! 'Why, of course' he always answered."

Becky and Bob got married after Becky had completed her first year of college at the University of Ohio. Bob worked at a local business, not far from where she was in school. They both had dreams, she to become a social worker and he to learn to fly.

"I always looked forward to getting married, but I knew I didn't want to be in the same role I saw my mother taking," Becky explains. "It seemed like Dad could do about what he wanted and Mom just fitted into his plans. I wanted our relationship to be more equal. I knew Mom and Dad loved each other, but our marriage would be different."

Bob recalls his similar intentions. "There was a lot of good in my family, but Mom didn't say a word about most things. I knew Becky wouldn't be that way! But I didn't know if it could be as 'equal' as Becky expected! I thought our roles would be pretty traditional, so when she began asking or even assuming that I would help her in the house, I faced a major adjustment, a drastic change. If my family had seen some of the things I was doing, they would have thought it strange and called me 'henpecked.'"

Without being aware of it, Becky and Bob soon began to fit into the roles they so disliked. Bob started his own business without consulting Becky. "I assumed it was my responsibility to handle the money, so I decided where it should go," Bob says. "Becky was more up–front with her feelings about things like this; my philosophy was to keep the peace at any price. I didn't want any friction in our marriage so I just kept my mouth shut. If I sensed we might disagree about something, I just didn't tell her and went ahead with those decisions without her. That's how Dad did it. He had the final word without needing to talk about things. But it wasn't working like it did with Mom and Dad. Becky cried a lot and I didn't know what to do with a wife who cried!"

"I wanted things to just be happy," Becky says. "I didn't realize that he wasn't telling me how he really felt. He seemed to agree with everything I said. I couldn't understand why he could talk so much to his friends when they came over, but he wouldn't talk with my college friends. I wasn't aware of his insecurities or that he felt I didn't really need him."

"I remember Becky driving down the road in her little car, looking so pleased with herself," Bob remembers. "She seemed to be thoroughly enjoying herself, like she was having a great time without me. I wasn't sure she needed me at all."

"But I didn't feel that way at all!" Becky counters.Even though she was involved with the National Honor Society and received a lot of recognition at school, in church and throughout the state, Becky was unable to feel truly valued.

As a young girl she had been sexually violated over a period of time by a relative. She kept the awful secret to herself until she met Bob and felt secure enough with him to tell him.

"I couldn't believe what I was hearing. She couldn't understand why I didn't get angry right away. But it was so awful and I didn't understand what my responsibility should be. I hurt terribly for her, but I didn't know what to do," Bob recalls his feeling of helplessness.

"All I wanted was for someone to take care of me and to hold me. I just wanted to be safe in my own home with my husband. I didn't know if I could ever really trust men, but Bob was different. I felt secure."

About a year and a half after they were married, Bob began to further question his own self–worth. Becky, on the other hand, was enjoying school, pursuing her goals, seeming to be "having a great time."

Then one day a "very needy person" came into Bob's life. "It felt so good to be needed," Bob admits sadly. "Becky was self-sufficient, it seemed she could do everything herself. I wasn't happy with myself, so I lit up when someone gave me a lot of recognition. I was extremely vulnerable and I made some very bad mistakes."

Becky was oblivious to what was going on. Bob determined to extricate himself from this other relationship, but didn't know how to tell Becky what had happened. Two thoughts tormented him. He knew very well the profound trauma Becky had experienced; now he had violated a sacred trust she had in him. And would she leave him once she knew?

"After church one day," Becky recalls, "we were driving home when Bob began to sob almost uncontrollably. He had stood to make a new commitment of his life that morning and I couldn't understand what was wrong. I didn't know why he had responded the way he did in church, although I thought it was nice.

"Then he began sobbing out the story, piece by piece. He couldn't tell me everything—just bits of it. The next few days are a blur, a nightmare. My dreams and hopes were crushed, broken. All my old hurts were revived with a vengeance. I was absolutely destroyed.

"When we got back to the apartment Bob continued to sob, clinging to my arms and begging me not to leave him. He also asked me not to tell anyone, although he did allow me to call his uncle, who was a pastor, for counseling. He told me I should forgive Bob and everything would be okay again. There was no way I could do that."

Bob also agreed that Becky could tell her parents. They re-acted with support for Becky, but also concern for Bob. They wanted to be sure that someone was with him all the time, even when he went to work, fearing that he might hurt himself. "I wanted to disappear and I wished I could die, although I never thought I'd be able to commit suicide," Bob says.

"Those days were awful. I don't remember a lot about them except how terrible I felt about what I had done and the over-whelming fear that Becky would leave me," Bob adds. "Becky has told me since some of the things that were going on then. I honestly don't remember."

"I remember everything," Becky says. "I didn't want him to leave, but I didn't want him there either. I couldn't stand him wanting to touch me or be close in any way. I hated the apart-ment because I knew she had been there. The strange thing is that I didn't cry—not much at all."

They recall together a lot of seesawing during those days. Sometimes Becky believed she could get over what had hap-pened and would leave for school in a fairly good mood. "I would think, maybe we're going to be all right after all," Bob remembers, "then she would come home and see me and lose it."

"Other times, I was the strong one and he would fall apart," Becky recalls. "I finally began to cry and cry and told my mom that I didn't think I could ever laugh and be happy again."

One day an aunt brought them some Recovery of Hope bro-chures. When they discovered it was a week–long event, as well as a Saturday morning session, they felt they were unable to afford the time away from school and work. But the family offered to cover the financial costs. Becky talked with one of her trusted professors who also encouraged her to go for help. So they found themselves enroute to another state, away from family, to work with people they had never met.

"We started getting silly on the way," Becky recalls. "We talked about going to this psychiatric hospital and all the stereo-typical stories about a place like that. In between we cried, both of us scared to death, yet believing it was the right thing to do. We knew we needed help and so here we were, headed for

Pennsylvania."

They laugh together now as they relive taking the psychological tests, both at tiny cubicles in a little testing room at the hospital. "These are stupid," Becky remembers saying. "What in the world do these have to do with our problems?"

"By Wednesday though, we were feeling much better, more comfortable and secure. We were learning a lot about ourselves and our marriage," Bob says. The Recovery of Hope intensive week involves a lot of homework—communication skills practice, reading and writing assignments. One assignment is to shop for a gift for each other. "Neither of us could figure out why we were to do this, but it turned out to be very significant," Bob says. "I realized that I had never bought Becky a dress even though I knew how important clothes were to her. It was brand new for me."

"I won't forget the wonderful surprise it was when I saw the beautiful dress Bob bought. I was feeling ugly and insecure but I suddenly felt good all over," Becky says smiling. "I bought him a silver necklace, something I knew he wanted as well, and he's still wearing it."

Although Becky and Bob made a lot of progress that week, some of the most difficult work was to follow. "We didn't want to go home again; there were too many things to face there. But we were different, too. We could talk about how we were feeling, even if it was painful, and we were learning to listen to each other," Becky says.

When they arrived at their apartment, they smelled fresh flowers and saw new plants. One room was newly wall–papered; there were new curtains with a bedspread to match. Becky's family had outdone themselves to welcome them home.

"We had a certain euphoria about all this," Becky recalls, "but it didn't last long. It was very difficult to be in that apartment. I wanted to move out right away, but we couldn't yet. We worried about a lot of things—would people find out about all this? Most people would have thought I was crazy to stay with Bob. At school the kids were talking about clothes and movies and I was trying to keep my life together. It was very difficult."

"I was afraid that even though we had worked hard and made

some good progress, Becky might still retaliate in some way, not that I would have blamed her," Bob says. "I was afraid that she would tear me down in front of people and tell everyone what an awful thing I had done." It never happened.

"Resuming intimacy of any kind was difficult for me," Becky says. "I was really down on myself. I kept remembering how hurt I had been, and that I would never stay if it happened again.

"Bob and I did a lot of talking and stayed in counseling, too. I eventually had to risk and to forgive God for permitting all this. I felt he had allowed it to happen when I was a child and now I was devastated again. That was hard. Seeing Bob change made it easier. He began to actually say what he was thinking and how he felt. Others saw the change in him, too. Even though I don't like to hear it, time has helped and the pain does get less and less."

"It was difficult to return home and be with my father again," Bob admits. "I had never had much of a relationship with him, and I was just beginning to finally feel better about myself. Then I would hear all these put–downs and demeaning things from him. It was hard for Becky to hear it too. We never have talked with my parents about our problems and counseling."

One of the things Becky and Bob decided was to ask that no one called Bob "Bobby," the family nickname for him. "When I heard his dad calling him that again, it really upset me," Becky remembers. "It seemed like he couldn't let his son grow up and be an adult. But Bob handled it very well, and I saw him as a mature man."

Becky and Bob have found that talking to other couples with similar experiences has been helpful. A network of couples exists who have been part of Recovery of Hope. They meet just to support and encourage each other. One of the ongoing issues for Becky has to do with forgiveness. "It's been good to talk to others who felt betrayed and hurt like I was and to find out what they did. I still have trouble, sometimes more than others, with hating her. It seems like I don't want to stop, but I know that some day I will."

Anxiety still emerges for Becky when Bob is late coming home or when he sees an attractive woman. "Some of those old feelings come up and I have to deal with them again. But now we can talk openly and I can ask for reassurance without feeling needy or inadequate. Bob volunteers lots of affirmation about me as a person; that's important to me. Recently when I initiated sex and Bob didn't respond, I was totally upset. But we talked about it and I was reassured that I'm loved and special. It works so much better to be honest about what's going on between us. When we observe other couples who just aren't dealing with each other in a healthy way, we know how far we've come."

"Our faith in God, our values and our love for each other have made us believe that even though these events in our lives were unspeakably painful, a lot of good has come from them. We've both changed and grown. We're different persons than we were when our marriage almost fell apart. It would have been a terrible loss had we given up on each other instead of working it out together," Bob say emphatically.

What issues might they be facing in their marriage if it hadn't been for the crisis? Says Becky with certainty, "I don't know, but I do know that we wouldn't be as close as we are—we wouldn't be best friends like we are now."

Becky recently graduated from college with top honors and is employed as a case worker, enjoying it all. Bob has only a few hours to go before receiving his pilot's license, with lots of dreams for further training. They have weathered a real crisis and agree that the roots of their marriage have grown deep and secure.

"We laugh a lot, we tease each other, and we have a lot of fun together," Becky says, "something I wasn't sure I could ever do again. We even know how to have good fights!"

"I was a little edgy when we began going through this story again," admits Bob, "but it's helpful to see how far we've come. And we both have a lot of dreams and hopes for the future. Who knows, we may have a couple of little guys or girls running around in flannel shirts, cowboy boots, big belts and buckles," smiles Bob.

Becky looks at his belt and says fondly, "I've got a long way to go with this guy!"

7

Building Walls

Sam drove a truck for years. Metaphors from those experiences weave through his account of his and Marie's marital journey. "There was a point in our marriage that I thought, 'What is the use of trying anymore?' It seemed that no matter what I did or didn't do, nothing ever changed. Our marriage was out of control. I felt like I was in my truck, speeding through a darkened tunnel with no end in sight."

Marie, with intense blue eyes and short graying hair, leans forward as she remembers. "I began to feel as if we had reached a place of no return and that things would only get worse, never better. We were middle–aged people; how would we ever live through our older years like this?

"We began to talk occasionally about separation. Each time we discussed it, however, it frightened me deeply. I had been taught that this was not an option for married people. Sometimes I wished I could prove that Sam had been involved in an affair so I could feel justified in leaving the marriage. A few times when he left on the truck, he said he would not be back. I recall coming home from work and looking in the closet to see whether he had taken his clothes.

"I finally decided that I would try to be happy by myself, fill my life with things I enjoyed and endure our marriage as best I could. I told Sam that if we separated, he would have to be the one to leave." But she recalls a great void in her life that never left.

Sam's story begins this way. "The first seven years of my life were empty of love and affection. I have no memory of my mother holding me, of her reading to me or telling me she loved me. She drank heavily and often had men other than my father in the house.

"I remember running into the house one day after I had cut my foot and I found her in bed with a man. Sometimes, after my father went to work at 3:00 in the afternoon, she would put my sisters and me to bed, without supper, and go out for the evening. I was only about six years old and was very frightened, knowing that I was the oldest and responsible for my sisters.

"When I was seven my parents separated and I didn't see my mother for 15 years. This was during World War II, and my father joined the Navy where he served for four years. I went to live with an aunt and uncle. When the war was over, my father came home for a short period of time and then he, too, disappeared." Sam pauses. "I'm sure my aunt and uncle loved me in the best way they could, but they had a growing family and were very busy with the farm. I soon felt like an extra, unwanted little boy with no family of his own."

Sam tells how he grew into an angry and rebellious adolescent. At age 16 he ran away from home and began drinking. By the time he was 20 he was serving his second term in prison. When it was time for parole, his aunt and uncle consented to have him come back to live with them. An old friend encouraged him to start attending church where he had gone as a young teen.

"It was there I first noticed Marie," Sam says with a brightness in his eyes and voice. "I didn't know it at the time but some of her friends had dared her to date me. I guess it really was a daring thing to do, considering my past life, and, after all, she was the preacher's daughter!"

For Sam it was love at first sight. They had good times together and he felt sure that Marie loved him, too. "I thought, now I finally have someone who will love me, and when she consented to marry me after two years of dating, my joy knew no bounds!"

Marie smiles at the contrast in their early years. "I grew up in a conservative Christian home. I knew that my parents loved us and they worked hard to support their family. But since my father was a preacher, he always made it clear that the work of the church came first in importance to him. He was often away at meetings of some kind or other. My mother kept things going at home in spite of chronic fatigue and occasional illness. She was the traditional submissive wife," Marie summarizes.

From as early as she can remember, Marie rebelled against some of the strict requirements of being a preacher's daughter, especially when she was reminded that she should be an example to others. She didn't like feeling different from her friends. She often wished she knew, even as a young child, what people who lived differently than she did believed and thought. Books, she says, became her escape. She read everything she could get her hands on, and as a teenager especially enjoyed romance stories. These stories of living happily ever after began to shape her ideas and expectations about marriage. It all seemed to happen so effortlessly.

"When I married Sam I thought he would be the means of my living happily ever after. I saw him as the way out of the restricted life I was living, and was only slightly disturbed by the fact that my parents did not approve of our marriage. Sam was so exciting and romantic to be with. I thought we would share everything, all our intimate thoughts, as well as home and bed. We would live to make each other happy," Marie says with rueful wisdom.

"I recognize now how little prepared I was for all that marriage involved," Sam confesses readily. "Somehow, I thought that having Marie love me would take care of any difficulties that might come. We were houseparents at a Children's Home and lived in a small apartment there. The work was extremely demanding and often overwhelming. I felt like I could relate to the children in a special way because I understood what it was like to be neglected and rejected. Soon I found it easier to be with them than to be with Marie. Even on our days off I played with the boys rather than being with Marie. We spent no time working on our relationship, and I was totally unaware of how hurt she felt about this."

After leaving the children's home with their own small daughter, Sam started working on a farm. Within a few years, they had two sons. He again found it easier to be out doing the farm work, which was unending, than to be with Marie, where there were also unending family responsibilities. "One reason I stayed away from home was because of my smoking habit. From the beginning I was dishonest about it and found excuses to run errands or not to take the boys with me so I could smoke without being seen. Marie told me it wasn't the smoking that bothered her as much as the dishonesty. But I continued being untruthful until she really began to mistrust me. I think it was an area of control I held on to and a way to get back at Marie for making me feel guilty."

Marie remembers those years vividly. "I began to feel early on in our marriage that Sam was angry with me, as though he was punishing me for something. I had no idea why he would feel that way, but I never tried talking to him about it."

Marie often felt that Sam didn't help with disciplining the children, but he remembered the harsh discipline he had received and did not want his children to fear him as he had his mother. He was afraid they would lose their love for him.

"I remember something that happened regularly on Sundays. When we came home from church I would hurry to help the children change into play clothes and would rush to get dinner on the table. I usually cooked a big dinner on Sundays," Marie says with some pride. "Sam would head down the road to talk with his friends at the service station until he thought dinner might be ready. I remember how upset the children and I got if he was late and we had to wait for him. He didn't need much of an excuse to get out of the house to smoke. I sometimes told him that if he wanted to smoke that was his decision, but would he please be open and honest about it. I was worried about the kind of impression this would have on the children," Marie recalls, still with some anger. "I imagined that if he was dishonest about this, he was dishonest about many other things. If he could lie to me about this, what else might he be lying about? After he became a truck driver, this began to bother me even more."

Marie remembers many times when Sam would call from some distant place to tell her he would be hours late. She wondered if he was telling the truth and allowed her imagination to run wildly. When he did get home, often exhausted and frustrated, she would question him angrily and accusingly, which only increased the hurt and alienation.

"For years my truck was my refuge," Sam admits. "I could walk out of a situation at home and leave Marie to solve the problems. I knew she resented this and it only added to the hostility between us, but it was much easier to leave."

Sam recalls one evening a few years ago when they were having a particularly difficult time with one of their children. "I did not, or rather *would* not, take charge of this crisis. It became more than Marie could handle. In desperation she got one of my guns, planning to take her life. My sons and I took the gun from her, but instead of remaining home to help work through the situation with her and our son, I did the one thing I was good at: I fled to the refuge of my truck.

"When I got back from the trip, we got into a heated argument about what had happened. Finally she yelled at me, cursed me and said, 'I wish you would have never entered my life.' I felt again like the little boy with no home of his own. I could not understand why she was so withdrawn from me. It seemed as if she was trying to turn the children against me as well. I could see no way out," Sam speaks with profound sadness.

There is an abandoned stone quarry filled with water not far from their home. One night when Marie was away, Sam lay in bed but could not sleep. He finally decided that if he were out of Marie's life, she could go on and find someone who would share responsibilities and care for her better than he could. He was so depressed and hopeless that he got out of bed with one intention. He would go to the quarry, jump in and no one would know what had become of him.

"Somehow I never made it to the quarry that night," Sam says with deep feeling. "I look back now and believe that God had better things in store for us, even though at the time I could see no hope for our marriage. Our relationship was like an iceberg, drifting into warmer waters, slowly disappearing. Soon there would be nothing left. Occasionally we talked about separation, but I couldn't imagine a life without Marie. I sincerely wished things could be different at home.

"I was often troubled about what our friends and family would say if they knew of our difficulties. So far we had done a good job of hiding things from them. People really thought well of us, and I felt even more like a hypocrite. I was overwhelmed with a sensation of speeding down the highway, having lost control of my truck which was about to crash."

Marie leans back in her chair, closing her eyes, remembering. "My fantasy about marriage had been only that, a fantasy. The real thing was quite different. Instead of intimacy and closeness, we had hostility and mistrust. And although these feelings surfaced early on, the responsibilities of our family seemed to accelerate our inability to deal with them. With this came a terrible, crushing sense of depression for me.

"I will never forget the night I tried to take my life. By then our children were teenagers and when they had problems, somehow I felt responsible for them. It all became too heavy for me to handle. I had failed not only as a wife but also as a parent. At that point I hated myself so much and felt so unable to deal with that I just wanted to die. The family saw what I was doing and restrained me, but I had lost control of myself. I had always perceived Sam as not being able to deal with problems and this was no exception. As he had done so often before, he escaped by leaving in his truck and one of our neighbors had to take me to a friend for help.

"I felt like I was being pulled into a deep, dark hole without any way to get out. I prayed for an accident. I thought of crashing the car and fantasized about other ways to take my life. I longed to share my feelings of despair with Sam but I was afraid he wouldn't care. The distance between us grew wider. It was as if I was on a train speeding away from him. Soon, I believed, I would never be able to find my way back. He didn't even seem to know I was in need of him, and I thought he was looking at me accusingly for not being able to control my depression. Sometimes he would say, 'Why can't you stop feeling sorry for yourself and get on with life?' Then I felt guilty because I couldn't.

"Because I had a lot of difficulty sleeping and would sometimes wake up shaking with fear, my doctor prescribed some medication for me. But the worst thing of all during this period of my life," Marie remembers, "was the feeling that God had turned his back on me. I couldn't pray because I felt he didn't hear me.

"A good friend thought I would benefit from seeing a counselor and I began to visit him regularly, but Sam ridiculed the doctor and my need of him. So although the therapy helped me keep my sanity, it did little to help our marriage.

Sam recalls how inadequate he felt in any number of ways. It seemed there was never enough money. "I could expect that almost every day Marie would complain about some financial need or other. It became much easier for me just to keep things bottled up inside. When she wanted to talk, I would sit in silence. If I did respond to her questions I would say, 'I don't know' or 'Do whatever you think.' I was trying to shift all the responsibility onto her. "What a relief it was to flee to my truck and get away from all the problems at home. The thrill and excitement of the open road gradually replaced some of the pain and hurt from our failing relationship."

Sam noticed that Marie was growing increasingly suspicious of him. He remembers calling one night from Virginia to tell her what time he would be home. He didn't know that he would be held up in traffic because of an accident ahead, which made him hours later than he had said. When he got home late that night, she was waiting up to question him.

"I often wondered why I had married someone who wanted to run my life. Many times I would strike out at her verbally and once when this happened she told me she was afraid of me. 'Don't be stupid, I would never hurt you,' I said, but deep inside I was afraid I might lose control and hurt her or do something I would always regret," Sam says.

"I felt he no longer loved or even cared about me or my needs and feelings.

We were building walls between us, both of us adding stones. Daily they became thicker and more impenetrable," Marie continues. "Many times I wondered in confusion and despair how we had come to this. I thought we had truly loved each other when we married. I remembered the good times we had had together and wondered if it was my fault that we had lost that part of our relationship. But any time I suggested to Sam that he accompany me for help, he refused. After all, he would say, it was my problem.

"So we went, year after year, unable to reach each other. I saw Sam as a closed up person. That's when I really began to wonder how in the world we would live through our older years together. Was there no way out?"

There came a turning point, however.

Sam describes the exact date and time of that "living hell." He was becoming increasingly frightened about their situation. Somehow he had a strong sense of urgency, that if he didn't do something, he would lose Marie. "That week in October, 1986, I kept getting the feeling that I was locked in a small room with no doors or windows to get out. Every day the room kept getting smaller until by the end of the week it seemed as if I was suffocating."

Sam and Marie went with a small group of friends to the mountains that weekend. They had an argument before they left and the trip there was quite uncomfortable. On Sunday morning, however, they went for a walk together. Sam could see the anger and pain in Marie's eyes and he began to realize how much he cared about her.

"I realized I didn't want to hurt her any more, but I didn't know how to change things. It seemed she no longer needed me. She had her job, her hobbies, her friends and her occasional classes that kept her busy. None of those things included me. We had become strangers living under the same roof, going our own ways. I couldn't stand it anymore. I thought maybe if I shared this great burden with my friends, they could help," Sam recalls.

A break came in the conversation the group was having and Sam remembers thinking, now or never. Even though Marie had told Sam she was not going to leave the marriage, he felt he had lost her. He asked God for courage to share his feelings.

"As we sat there talking with each other, one side of me said, 'Don't tell them,' but the other side insisted, 'You must if anything is to change.' That battle raged inside me as I sat unable to speak. Finally, deep within myself, I felt the strength of a gentle urging, assuring me of the rightness of what I wanted to share. It was a voice encouraging me to be honest and admit our problems. I looked across the table at Marie and knew she was a remarkably special person to have stayed by me for the past 28 years," Sam says softly.

"I'll never forget that morning," Sam continues. "It was a beautiful, bright day, full of sunshine. We were sitting around a picnic table and there was a pond in the background. I finally told the group I had something to say. I began to pour out my heart about how much I wanted our marriage to work and things to change."

Marie remembers that morning too, and how she interrupted him angrily, saying, "I've heard that story before and I don't believe it, and I'm not going to sit here and listen to this." She recalls getting up from the table, and storming up to the cabin.

"That hurt me a lot," Sam admits. "I remembered the feeling of driving my truck through a dark tunnel with no end in sight, but this time I knew I had to keep on going. As I look back now, I know if Marie had stayed with the group, I would not have been as free to share with them. Someone eventually suggested we should try Recovery of Hope. I agreed, and that is a decision I will never regret."

After a long time, Marie rejoined the group and Sam told her about his decision. Her reaction was total disbelief. Her therapist had suggested they attend Recovery of Hope and Marie had placed brochures around the house where Sam could see them, but nothing had happened. She finally said in a derisive voice, "I will believe you are sincere when we are sitting in a Saturday morning session."

Marie had often asked Sam to enter counseling with her, but he always dropped the subject and wouldn't refer to it again. "I guess that's why I was so cynical and angry the morning he began sharing with our friends about our problems and how he wanted them to change. I shouted at him in anger because I didn't believe he was sincere. When I came back from the cabin Sam was in tears and told me he would do whatever we could agree on to change our relationship. Suddenly it felt to me as if we had knocked a hole through the wall we had built and were looking through it at each other."

One evening Sam astonished Marie by saying that he believes he has always mistrusted women because he had been rejected by his mother as a small child."Suddenly a light turned on for me!" Marie exclaims as she remembers that moment of insight for her. "I realized why I had felt from the beginning of our marriage that he was punishing me for something. His feelings toward women in general affected his feelings toward me as well. I knew the story of how he had been neglected and given to someone else to raise, but I never thought before about how it might surface for him all these years later. It was such a relief to know it was not something I had done that brought on his anger and mistrust." Sam made the phone call to register for the initial session of Recovery of Hope and Marie remembers what a signal she believed that to be, that he seemed determined to change. She feared, however, that at the last minute he would change his mind. After all, he had trampled on her hopes before. She remained quite skeptical, prepared for any pain that might come.

"I discovered that I was not certain I wanted to go. Now that Sam was finally ready to get help, and even excited about it, I wanted to hurt him like he had hurt me before by refusing to go with me for help. But deep down inside I sensed a warm, glowing feeling spreading. Maybe Sam did care more than I knew. Maybe if we worked together we could change our relationship." Marie remembers the anticipation she had.

A few weeks after attending the Saturday morning session, Sam and Marie entered the Recovery of Hope intensive week of marital therapy. They describe the hard work they did during that week.

"I learned a lot," Sam recalls. "I began to see, much to my surprise, what influence our childhood years have on our lives and how we bring these things into our marriages. I saw that we can change our destructive ways of relating and can rebuild and learn to walk together. I saw how much my negative feelings about my parents affected the way I related to Marie. I discovered I didn't even like myself and had felt like my decisions and ways of doing things were always inferior.

"But," Sam continues, "I also learned that I could forgive my parents and choose to go from here. I had to let go of the past and live in the present. I saw that when things didn't go right, I would just crawl back into the past and hide. But I needed to learn to face things and share my thoughts and feelings with Marie, that she was a friend with a listening ear who wanted to understand where I was coming from. I saw that I was a worthwhile person with whom Marie wanted to share her life. We could change!"

Marie agrees. "That week changed our lives. We began to understand all the things we brought into our marriage. I saw Sam as a person who needed me as much as I needed him. I came to see that even with the many years of hostile feelings built up between us, we could begin again."

Slowly, often painfully, in the weeks and months after their intensive week, Sam and Marie continued to build their relationship. After 28 years of marriage, old habits and patterns are not easy to change. But they now had new tools to work with, a new understanding of themselves and each other, and a renewed love for and commitment to each other.

"I had always liked to think that most of what was wrong with our marriage was Sam's fault," Marie admits. "I learned that my demandingness and insistence that we always do things my way only caused Sam to retreat further away from me into silence. When I heard him say by his words and actions that he truly wanted our marriage to work, I began to trust him and to share my own deep, personal feelings with him. But I found I needed to make a conscious effort to change my attitude toward Sam.

"One thing I learned that I need to be constantly reminded of—you act your way into a change of feelings; you don't wait until you feel just right before you change your actions," Marie says.

Continued professional counseling and becoming part of a couples' group have been important elements in Sam's and Marie's recovery. The counseling helps on those occasions when they find themselves falling into the same old patterns as before.

"I was uncomfortable in the couples' group at first," Marie admits. "But we found that others face such similar problems and we could help each other deal with them. The experience of being open about my pain has been a freeing one for me. It's as if I opened myself up and the pain left and flew away," Marie says about her experiences.

"Sometimes I have to admit that I feel discouraged and wonder what's the use of going on, but the support of the group and other friends has helped to keep us on the right track," Sam adds.

He continues, "I decided several months ago to quit truck driving, something I thought I would never do. I was giving up my refuge, my means of escape from things I didn't want to deal with. This was a hard adjustment for me, but I knew Marie meant more to me than my truck did."

Marie talks about how she has experienced the switch. "Sam's decision to quit driving truck meant a major adjustment for me. I was used to going my own way without him. But his commitment to the rebuilding of our relationship, which led to the job change, spoke loudly to me and I liked what I heard!"

Sam adds, "Recently I came to work for the same company Marie does. It feels like we've come full circle. We began our marriage by working together, first at the Children's Home and then on the farm. This time we are determined to use this to bring us closer together."

While they do spend much more time together, Marie acknowledges that she continues to work at building trust. "I must admit that I still tend to keep deep personal things to myself," she says. "But each occasion of sharing makes it easier for me the next time. My early dreams of closeness and intimacy are finally becoming a reality."

But Sam and Marie have had to face some painful experiences. "When I made the decision years ago not to leave Sam, I did it partly because I was not willing to give up the good times we had together as a family. In spite of our great difficulties, we did have fun with our children and they enjoyed coming home, laughing around the dinner table, telling jokes, playing games and talking. We could almost pretend that all was well with us," Marie explains.

"When we were feeling so good about our new relationship we thought our children would be happy for us and we would become even closer as a family. But sadly, it has not been that way. Things have changed. They rarely come home these days. We have not seen one of them for more than two years. Both our sons have had difficulty with their marriages. They have made choices that we do not understand. It's been hard for us not to blame each other," Marie continues.

The anguish they carry because of their family situation makes it difficult for them to keep focused on each other. "We have to work at helping each other through the pain since we deal with it differently," Marie says. "Ironically, I stayed with Sam because of the family. We don't really have the family anymore, but now in a truer sense than ever before, we have each other."

"It is hard not to blame each other for the mistakes our children have made," Sam agrees, "but we believe if we had not begun the rebuilding of our relationship when we did, our marriage would not have survived the storms of the past few years."

"I had thought, in my despair, that a happy and fulfilling relationship with Sam would never be. But I learned that I can change if I want to, and with my husband's help. He is my friend and, instead of the hopelessness I felt, I have real joy," Marie says with contentment.

One thing Sam and Marie have come to enjoy is taking walks together. "We have a little–travelled country road close to our home," Sam says. "The peace and quiet there fills me with contentment and admiration for the very special person who is walking beside me. It's a good time to share what's on our minds and just to be together. It's so much better than falling back into the old patterns of either angry silence or shouting matches!

"My feelings of driving through a dark tunnel with no end in sight, or being about to crash, are mostly gone. Now it feels like I've driven the truck safely home and parked it. Home with Marie—that's where I belong."

"Many of the walls we had built are still there, but stone by stone, we are breaking them down. Now we can see over them to each other," Marie adds.

8

It Still Hurts

"I think I was about four and a half years old," Jennie begins. "My dad had come home drunk—again—and he made me and my younger brothers and sister sit in a row on the sofa. I remember it was very cold and snowing outside. We lived in a little trailer house. My mother was in the bedroom and my father was yelling at her—I don't know what about—and he got a stack of empty milk cartons and took them to the bedroom. Then he set them on fire, apparently hoping to burn my mother. I don't remember all that happened, except how frightened I was and how much I hated my father and how he made us sit and watch him do all this."

Uncertainties and trauma were her daily companions in this chaotic home. Her mother became pregnant with Jennie at age 15. "It was what we would call date rape now. It was in the '50s and there was apparently no choice but to get married. There was no discussion. Your parents made you. My mother said she was too scared to tell anyone about the rape. No one would have believed her or else she would have been blamed for it.

"By the time my mother was 25, she had eight children. I remember on any number of occasions my father forcing her onto the floor, making her have sex with him and I saw it all. If she went to her mother (my grandmother) for help, she would say, 'You made your bed, now lie in it.'

"We lived poorly. There were three beds for 10 people, holes in the wall, no wallpaper. I don't remember happy times. All the dirty laundry went behind a door in the kitchen and we had to dig for what we wanted, clean or not. There was no shower or tub, only a washbowl."

Phil, on the other hand, came from a very stable home. "Everyone knew what was expected of them and we just did it!" Phil says emphatically. "Being a conscientious productive worker and being a good manager were all–important to my parents. We were very regular churchgoers, although there was never much joy or spontaneity connected with it. It was all completely different from Jennie's home. It was hard for me to understand that people could actually live that way."

"It was totally different," Jennie agrees. "Phil's mom was always there for them. I don't know what that would be like. Since I was the oldest in my family, I had to take care of the others. My mother took odd jobs because Dad was gone, working on the railroad and so I took over the household. Mom was really kind–hearted—she always gave to others even though we were terribly poor. We ate potatoes a lot!" Jennie laughs. "Once when we did have meatloaf, Dad threw it out in the back yard because he was mad about something.

"He was mean and evil. He never went to the hospital with my mom when the babies were born. I think she lost one or two, but I'm not sure. When you're living like we did, it's a matter of surviving from day to day. I missed a lot of school during those years as well."

Jennie remembers some especially traumatic events. "I was often asked to baby–sit for neighbors, too. I was only 11 when I went to stay with a neighbor's child while her mother was in the hospital having another baby. I was in bed sleeping when her husband came home drunk. I was really frightened. He soon had me on the floor and raped me. I remember his hands and the huge ring with a big stone that he was wearing. He kept hitting me on the side of the face with it until I almost lost consciousness.

"When I finally got home I told my mother about it, but rather than the comfort and care I so desperately needed, she gave me a beating. This man was her best friend's husband. I think now that she didn't know what else to do. She was afraid for me and must have felt that somehow I was beginning the cycle all over again. But then I didn't understand at all. I thought I was being punished for something that was not my fault," Jennie remembers with great sadness.

"It was not unusual for us children to go to school with marks on our bodies, usually where they didn't show, but the school officials said that unless there were severe marks, they could do nothing. So we all suffered in silence and tried to survive the best we could.

"The first time I saw my mom try to stand up for herself or to retaliate was when Dad came home drunk and tried again to force her to have sex. She was ironing and she used the hot iron to keep him away, burning him on his side. He ran out that night and eventually moved in with another woman.

"Now as an adult I realize what a disconnected family I am part of. My uncles and aunts and grandmother lived next to us on both sides of our house and across the street as well. They all knew what was going on in our home, but no one stepped forward to help. They had to know. They could hear the yelling; they could see what my father was like and how he treated us children and my mother. It seems so odd how they were all family and lived so close, and yet we had no connections. When we would see each other in the neighborhood we acted as though all that was going on was normal," Jennie remarks.

"My maternal grandmother's stories sounded almost like my own mother's story. She, too, was surrounded by affairs, abuse and all kinds of chaos, but no one seemed to care."

Phil listens, shaking his head as he tries to imagine aloud what that would have been like. "Even though I've heard Jennie describe all this before, it's still hard to believe."

"Then one day," Jennie recalls, "I don't know what happened, but my mom had all she could take. I remember it was late at night and she got a call. I don't know who it was from. Dad was living with another woman at the time. Mom went out by herself and I don't know who she saw or where she went or what she did, but when she came back she was a different person. She had apparently gone over the edge. She just sat in a chair and stared. She became completely dysfunctional.

"During that time I went to school only one or two days a week because someone had to take care of the three little children. The youngest was only a year old. I tried to tell the officials at the school why I was absent. They responded by sending out truant officers and police and people from the Children's Bureau. But they never sent anyone to really investigate what was going on. They said they couldn't do anything until Mother did something that was really hurtful to herself or those around her.

"I was only 13 then, going on 30, I guess," Jennie reflects on her adolescence. "I didn't really have a childhood. I was not only responsible for my brothers and sisters, but my mother as well. She just sat and stared—for weeks, as I remember. And then one day she gave me a note to take to Dad who was working part–time as a bartender. I didn't know what the note said, but he came back to the house before long. Mom pretended to come over to him to give him a hug and a kiss, but she had a big kitchen knife and stabbed him in the chest, and then stabbed herself over and over again." Jennie pauses as she remembers seeing the horror of it all.

"He ran out the door screaming and dropped over in front of the house. I remember ambulances coming for both of them. Eventually Mom was committed to a psychiatric hospital for treatment. Dad died in the hospital a couple months later. He was only 32." Jennie pauses and then comments, "I've often thought what a terrible waste."

Jennie remembers attending the funeral of her father just before Christmas. "I wrote a note and put it in his coat pocket before they closed the coffin. In the note I asked why he couldn't have been kind to us. I said I wished he could have loved us. I remember feeling how cold his body was and thought to myself that he had no blood in his veins, He felt just like he had been when he was alive."

Jennie, 13, was left with the task of caring for seven younger siblings. It was almost impossible for her to continue in school. Her grandmother "checked in on us" every once in while, but the majority of the care was hers to provide.

"I remember that one of my biggest concerns was what to do for my brothers and sisters for Christmas. We didn't have any-thing. Someone brought us some candy and the kids ate it all and I was so upset, I lined them all up on the couch and made them sit there!" she recalls with winsome sadness. "Then some people got together and set up a gift collection at the store with gifts for all of us. I remember how good that felt."

Soon thereafter a truant officer came to call again. "Someone must have turned us in because there were people who came from the Children's Bureau and began dividing us out to different foster homes. They assured us that we would always be in touch and could see each other and that it would be best for everyone, but all of us were really upset," Jennie remembers painfully.

"I'll never forget the day they came and began to take my brothers and sister away, one by one, with their meager belongings. The most difficult thing was when my sister cried and begged me not to let them take her." She pauses, lost for a bit in the agony of those moments.

"When they forcibly took her, she yelled back at me, 'I hate you for letting this happen,' but I couldn't do anything." Jennie stops again, full of the helplessness, the anger, the fears and the profound trauma of that moment as a 13–year–old.

"When I turned 14, I knew they were coming to take me to a foster home, too. I had been living off and on with my grandmother, but that wasn't really a good arrangement. I was determined not to go to a foster home, so I ran away and lived in a bungalow with a girlfriend whose mother was gone most of the time. There were men in and out of that house, and all kinds of things going on that I don't even want to remember. It was a bad scene," Jennie says, trying to forget. "But eventually they came for me and I was placed in a home. My attitude was that no one was going to tell me what to do," she recalls.

"I was transferred to four different homes in four years. I never got to see my brothers and sister. In fact, it seemed they did everything to keep us apart. All their promises were forgotten. School was really difficult for me. I had missed so much and didn't really care if I went or not.

"I most remember, as an older foster child, just wanting to be loved and accepted. For some reason it seemed my foster parents never had enough patience to build a trusting relationship. I know that part of the difficulty was my own feelings because I had a hard time trusting anyone. Although it seemed that case workers came around like flies, they were overworked and underpaid and nothing really ever seemed to come out of their efforts.

"My brothers and sister have all had hard times growing up. They have all had a lot of problems, even the very little ones who were in fairly stable homes from the beginning." Jennie pauses and comments rather matter–of–factly, "So, the dance goes on." Jennie looks at Phil and smiles and says, "Except for me."

Phil picks up the story. "My dad told me one day that there was an attractive girl working at the restaurant close to our home. I decided to go and investigate! I was 19 and Jennie was just 15, but I liked what I saw. I guess I was pretty bashful because after we talked a while, Jennie suggested it would be fun to go bowling and I thought it was a great idea. But I found out that she was also seeing someone else. I must have wanted to learn to know her pretty much because I wasn't deterred by that!"

Jennie remembers her reaction, "I thought Phil was pretty young since I hadn't really dated many guys under 25, but Phil was so different from any of them."

Jennie and Phil reminisce about their wedding plans, the fun, the excitement, yet some of the clouds that hung over them. "My parents couldn't bless this marriage," Phil explains. "They thought she was 'unworthy of our family name.' After they called her 'trash,' I chose not to work with Dad. It would have been far too difficult and confining. I had had enough of that."

Jennie recalls her prenuptial jitters. "My foster mother would-n't listen to me when I said I didn't know if I wanted to get married, that I wasn't sure I was ready. I felt I was putting my life into someone else's hands and that was scary. I kept hearing in my mind, 'You made your bed, now lie in it.' But I knew Phil was different. I had never known a man like him. I knew he loved me, and that I had finally found someone I could trust, someone who loved and accepted me, even though he knew all the things about me that he did.

"But I couldn't shake the nagging fears that came from all those things in my experience that had been out of my control.

On the other hand, when you're at the mercy of foster homes and case workers, it's difficult not to put up a strong front. I had to do that to survive! I didn't know how to identify all the colliding forces within me at that time, let alone deal with them."

Jennie talks about the first years of their marriage with deep feeling. "It took me a long time to feel okay about myself. I worked so hard in so many different ways to be accepted and to belong. Sometimes Phil perceived me as being so self-sufficient that I didn't need anything or anyone."

Phil agrees with Jennie's analysis. "I remember often trying to reassure her that I loved her and that this would last. She almost went overboard trying to prove that she was worthwhile and deserving. She wouldn't have had to do that," Phil says. "I loved her for who she was—and still do," he adds with obvious fondness.

"I didn't always show her as clearly as I could have though. I began to take her for granted, forgetting to be sensitive to her needs and feelings. After all, I had brought all the baggage from my own background, with expectations of how she ought to be as a wife. As I tried to provide security and stability for her, I started to fit into the traditional role my father had when I was growing up," Phil says.

"I had always tried to take Jennie's ideas and wishes into all our decision-making, but gradually I made more and more decisions without her, especially those that had to do with finances. This was particularly true when I made the decision to move and build a new house. I didn't really consult her about it at all. It was more of a unilateral decision. I know now it was wrong. I couldn't or didn't want to know what an impact this would have on Jennie," Phil says with real regret. "I guess I thought once we were in a lovely, brand new home, she would agree it was a good move."

The difficulties this decision triggered surfaced with a vengeance. "It was really hard for me when Phil decided on his own that we were moving and building a new home," Jennie says. "I've come to realize that it wasn't the actual move that started the wedge in our marriage, but the fact that I wasn't included in the decision to move or in designing the new house. We had always shared decision–making and I thought we had always been close, but now I was extremely angry. I felt my husband betrayed me and was pushing me aside."

She continues emphatically, "Besides, because Phil was at work, I was the one who had to be responsible for making sure the contractor and other workmen got their jobs done. I strongly resented this. It wasn't my decision and I didn't want to be there. I was always screaming, 'You'll do what you want anyway,' if he asked for my opinion. To which he replied, 'You'll never be satisfied no matter what I do. I can't please you!'"

These events resurrected feelings which Jennie thought were gone. Phil and the children and the home they had established together had been her security. Now she felt her world slowly crumbling.

"Little by little I started closing doors as Phil made more and more decisions without me. On top of this, Phil's family thought we were building a new home because of my control and drive, and his mother let me know that there was no reason for such a big beautiful house to be built. All the while Phil sat silent and didn't come to my defense. He didn't tell them that it was his decision to build, not mine," Jennie states.

"I felt cold, angry and empty. Those feelings of never being good enough for his family swept down over me again. He used to tell me that it was my imagination. But I remembered being told I came from trash and would always be trash. I remembered that his mom said she would pray for Phil but not for me," Jennie says with great emotion.

It was a difficult time for both of them. Jennie, dealing with her old feelings; Phil falling into a role he had grown up with— the man is in charge. "My hope was that Jennie would see that, in spite of the mistakes I had made, I still loved her deeply, that there was nothing she could do to change my love for her. But I was really afraid," Phil recalls.

The distance and alienation continued, even though they both put on a good front for family and friends. Jennie particularly withdrew from Phil emotionally and physically. She asked him to leave for a short time and he felt helpless in knowing what to do to regain the closeness he felt they once had. Jennie remembers that she truly didn't know if their marriage would survive these crises. "I didn't know if we could trust one another again."

Jennie was again living through the painful realities of being the child of a severely disrupted, abusive, alcoholic family. She had learned well to deny her feelings, not to trust others, not to have needs, to believe that problems were her fault, and that she was not entitled to anything good. Although in many ways she had moved far beyond these to a healthier view of herself, the current crisis had surfaced her old ways of thinking.

"I had to choose to believe again that I was entitled to be happy and content, and that my feelings and ideas were worthy of consideration. As the child of an alcoholic, it was ingrained in me that I never deserved anything," Jennie says with deep understanding. "As far as our marriage went, I knew that I had made a vow before God and I couldn't walk away from that promise, even though I was trying to justify myself in doing that."

Phil continues, "We had to confront some mercilessly difficult issues. The problems just didn't go away. Counseling helped, and we both had strong, however shaken, faith."

The journey to healing and reconciliation was hard for both of them. They agreed to confront not only themselves but each other and what had brought them to this place. They found learning to listen to each other, and to trust the other all over again, the most difficult tasks.

"One breakthrough came during a communication exercise in Recovery of Hope. We had to listen to one another and say to the other person's satisfaction what we heard. We both assumed so many things about what the other was meaning, and that had become a real block to reconciliation. We have to truly work on understanding what the other person is saying, listening with our hearts and not just our ears!"

Phil and Jennie continue to work at reconciliation and their marriage. "It's hard labor," Phil admits, "but the struggles can be so rewarding!"

"It's difficult as an adult not to try to prove yourself to others," Jennie continues. "I can't allow myself to be weak. I still want to belong so badly. I still depend a lot on the approval of others and do a lot more than I would have to do. It's as though I have to earn the approval of others, as though I'm not entitled to anything just because I am me. I used to struggle a lot with whether I was good enough for Phil. That's not quite so acute any more. I know I am not dependent on others for my self–worth and I do care for myself more than I used to. But it's a lonely road for people like me. I don't know if it ever stops being lonely."

Jennie and Phil have now been married for nearly 20 years, filled with both good times and hard. They have poured themselves into making a stable and pleasant home, Phil with his good job and steady ways, Jennie with her creativity. "It's the one thing I thank my Dad for. I inherited his artistic ability."

9

Systems and Themes: Teacher - Learner

Not only do spouses bring their roles from their families of origin to the marriage, they may also bring their "positions" from their chosen vocations. Consider Seth and Elaine who fell into a "teacher-learner" theme.

"After we were married Seth spent five years in graduate school," Elaine begins. "I remember sitting on the porch one day thinking, this is no marriage. I want out of this situation. He is married to his briefcase and all he needs me for is making meals, doing laundry and sex."

Although Seth was kind to her—always remembering birthdays and anniversaries—she never felt special to him, or anyone else.

"While I was growing up, my mother discovered an effective way to get me to do what she wanted. She told me I should be ashamed of myself whenever I did something that didn't please her, or that she thought made her look bad. I took it all to heart and made it my goal in life to learn what people wanted, to be compliant and never to make waves. Never again did I want to experience the terrible pain of my mother telling me to be ashamed of myself.

"A lot of who I was died along the way. I didn't dare to form my own opinions; after all, maybe I didn't know enough and would be criticized. I didn't dare to do things people disapproved of. I didn't give myself permission to be myself. Instead I functioned as an extension of whoever the other important person was in my life. When I married a therapist, I figured it was no use disagreeing with him. Focusing on the children helped me feel needed but I knew little pleasure in life; my skies were usually gray.

"On occasion Seth would say, 'Why don't you think more positively?' It seemed so simple to him, which only added to my not feeling understood. And then there was the public image we had to maintain!"

Their way of relating began to spill over into other areas of family life as well. Although the "house was littered with parenting books," Elaine felt pressured to agree with what Seth said in the children's presence, even though she believed he was relating to their daughter in a way that was driving her further from them all the time.

"I wanted so desperately for everyone to be happy," Elaine remembers, "but I didn't have the inner strength to disagree with him. After all, he was the professional counselor. In fact, lots of times I felt like a 'case' that he had to figure out. He seemed to know all the answers; he made the rules."

This teacher–learner relationship came out in other ways. "We both decided that we needed to get out and do things together more," Elaine says. "We lived in North Carolina where there were wonderful places to bicycle. So we bought two new 10–speed bikes, each with a child carrier on them. We took the children along and I thought, 'This is really going to be fun!' But I vividly recall the pain I felt when Seth insisted that to really get the most out of this, 'aerobic exercise value' he called it, we had to ride much faster than I wanted. He rode far ahead of us, and my sauntering along seemed to have no value. He thought he knew best about everything, from buying furniture to how we should go on walks."

Seth picks up the story. "For many years I didn't know Elaine was hurting about our relationship. I thought I was a good husband. I realized that at times she was depressed and that she sometimes criticized things that seemed trivial to me, but I didn't understand why that was necessary.

"I said that a counselor would just get us to talk to each other, so I suggested that we take time regularly on our own to do just that. We did, but the underlying problem did not go away. I was hurt when she was finally able to tell me that she felt I understood her only with my head," Seth recalls.

Seth and Elaine moved to Greensboro, and he soon became involved in a highly successful practice. Elaine describes what it was like to gain enough strength to seek help from someone else. "Asking for help when your husband is a professional counselor is not easy. It seemed all the therapists we knew in Greensboro were either colleagues of Seth's or his consultants.

"I remember the day when with fear and trembling I called to make an appointment with a counselor, hoping to just leave a message and have her call back later—but she was in. That was the beginning of facing myself. The process was long and slow, but for the first time in my life, I felt deeply understood and accepted. I began in that place of safety to give myself permission to be real, to own the feelings and longings and disappointments I had. Facing one problem brought more to the surface. I felt like a fly trapped in a huge spider web, each hurt being one strand of the web. Thanks to the counselor who never saw it as hopeless, the web lost its grip on me, one strand at a time.

"Experiencing acceptance in counseling became a bridge to knowing in a deep way that God loves, forgives and accepts me, despite my failures. That, in turn, became the basis of my worth and life," Elaine explains.

Seth continued to see his actions as "pretty good" and defended them quite well. "But the relief I was gaining with the counselor was enormous," Elaine recalls. "Someone actually did not put the blame on me, and took seriously what I said."

Seth remembers the process well. "I finally came to realize that I couldn't change Elaine. Even though I was jealous of the counselor and her ability to understand Elaine, I also trusted her as she worked with Elaine. And, I knew I had some changing to do, too."

Pain flowed both ways as they learned what each had contributed to the difficulties. Cast in a new role, Seth began to see how he responded to Elaine's feelings. "When she told me that she was hurt or upset about something, I would imply that she need not and should not feel that way. I honestly thought she would be better off if she just changed her way of thinking and became more like I thought she should be. What I failed to realize was that I was criticizing her for feeling hurt."

Seth suggested that they audiotape the sessions. That led to raw reality for him. "When I heard myself on tape, I became aware of how critical I sounded when I responded to Elaine's feelings with advice. Time after time I heard Elaine tell me something painful she had experienced and each time I braced myself, sure that I wouldn't respond that way again. But as I listened I heard myself repeating the pattern. I couldn't believe it," Seth shakes his head remembering.

"When I finally learned how to listen (you would think I would have known how!) with the intent of understanding rather than of teaching her something, or changing her, we could talk, often for hours. I was discovering some painful facts about myself that I needed to face."

Seth recalls listening to Elaine express a concern one Sunday afternoon. "Rather than trying to change her way of thinking, I just accepted what she said. To my amazement, without my help, she began to think optimistically and courageously about several troublesome areas. I realized I did not have to fix her up.

"I also found that when she said something that hurt me, I didn't have to defend myself. I made another amazing discovery—when I don't defend myself, I just feel hurt for a while—but it doesn't kill me! I can actually reflect on what she says without having to defend myself."

Elaine explains, "I began to see that by hiding my true thoughts and feelings from myself and from others, because I feared rejection, I was deeply wronging both my husband and myself.

"Sometimes I still act like a little shamefaced girl, but I'm aware that I can choose to be a woman. And when I see that Seth is willing to take a more honest look at who he is, I gather a lot of hope for our continually growing relationship."

Seth and Elaine both became willing to try new ways of relating. "I had to face the truth that Elaine does a lot of things better than I do, that I can learn from her. It still hurts when she sees things about me that need changing, but now she tells me and we can talk about it. How else will I ever learn?" Seth asks.

10

A Fairy Tale Gone Awry

The story of Vincent and Fran could very well begin, "Once upon a time..." She had been reared in a difficult and unhappy home environment. She tried to change the way things were by being a "good girl," by pleasing everyone but herself, by ignoring her own fears, longings and disappointments. But in time she began to believe that perhaps she didn't deserve to be happy, that she was not entitled to contentment.

Enter Vincent, from a respectable family, full of love and the promise of care her father had never provided. He was her answer to prayer and the fulfillment of her dreams.

Vincent was equally proud of his new love. She was beautiful; she made him proud to be with her. Now he had both a good job and a promising marriage. But before the marriage was very old, Vincent began to feel that he could not meet all of Fran's expectations and needs. "Turning the world upside down for her was not enough, but I kept all those things inside. It was hard for me to talk with my young bride."

Now a lovely graying woman, Fran talks about those early years and her expectations. "My husband was to be a real Prince Charming. He would make me the center of his life, pay a lot of attention to me and do everything he could to make me happy so I would never have to hurt again. He would be kind and tender, yet strong and protective. I even fantasized about how he would look—a combination of Tyrone Power and John Wayne! I would feel loved for the rest of my life and we would live happily ever after, not unlike Cinderella."

Fran's father was an alcoholic. "When folks asked my mother

when my father started drinking, she would say, 'Right after Fran was born.' What Mother failed to add was that it was during the Depression, that my father had lost his job and, consequently, his self-respect and was unable to face life without alcohol."

Fran heard a message that became a powerful influence in her life: she was responsible for her father's alcoholism and the subsequent disintegration of the family. "When he was sober, he was warm and loving. When drunk, he was mean and rejecting. I never knew from one day to the next whether he would be a Dr. Jekyl or Mr. Hyde. The uncertainty was unbearable. I felt unloved, insecure and unimportant.

"My mother was sensitive and after those frequent, sometimes violent, arguments she would run to her room, shut the door and weep. She often told me she wished she could die. I felt frightened and unloved by her as well; I couldn't understand *her* pain and fear. So I tried to be utterly compliant. Even as an adult I would get angry when Mother told friends and family how good I was because I used to say, 'Oh, all right,' no matter what I was asked to do. But I held the anger inside, as well as my other longings and disappointments."

To Fran Vincent looked like the person who could rescue her from all the pain and fill all her needs. "He made decisions without vacillating, and I was certain I had found a man who could be trusted to love and care for me," Fran says.

"Fran expected me to stay at home with her all the time when I was not working," Vincent remembers. "The more she nagged me, the more I wanted to get away. I liked sports but, even though she knew how important those events were to me, she would find reasons why I couldn't be gone. Sometimes she needed so much attention or extended conversation, especially about her feelings, that I began to feel smothered with all that focus on our relationship. I couldn't meet all her needs, nor could I explain how *I* was feeling. Gradually a cold wedge crept between us."

Vincent became more and more involved in work, where there was also a lot of pressure. "Fran said the only reason I was making it in the business was because my dad owned it and that

I was riding on his coattails. She seemed to give me no credit for all my hard work, and I felt like I was working my tail off. It just became easier to work harder and stay later on the job, because at least I felt important there."

"Our first child was a girl, and I idolized her," Fran speaks with obvious affection. "She became the central focus of my life, taking the place in my heart that I thought my husband would have. I know he felt rejected, but instead of sharing his pain with me, he took it out on the baby and a triangle was formed that further distanced us from each other.

"Our daughter learned early to get what she wanted from her daddy by appealing to me. When I interceded for her, Vincent resisted. Then I withheld love, affection or sex until he complied. Conversely, if Vincent didn't get what he wanted from me, he withheld things from her. I felt like the rope in a tug–of–war, torn between my allegiance to him and my love for our daughter. This pattern continued even when our other children came along. As time went by, the distance between Vincent and me grew more and more unbearable until I felt overwhelmed with loneliness."

Vincent remembers feeling that the new baby got all of Fran's love while he got none. "I needed Fran so much. I was lonely and felt unimportant to her, like I was only good for bringing home the pay check. It seemed we were caught in a vicious cycle—I was manipulating to get away and she was trying to control what I did and where I went.

"Sometimes I tried to be useful around the house, but it seemed no matter what I did, it wasn't enough or the right things. She didn't seem to appreciate the security I was providing; she never said anything to build me up. But I couldn't talk to her about my feelings. So I began to act out what I couldn't talk about.

"I didn't help with the children but I did criticize how she handled them. I put them down instead of praising them. I took Fran for granted and took advantage of her. I expected her to be like my mother had been. She supported my dad, even when he was wrong and did not deserve it. What I got in return were tears and a chewing out.

"There were times when I tried to put my arms around her and wanted to say how sorry I was for some things, but I was afraid she would reject me, or criticize the way I was going about it—her usual pattern. Her criticism began to sound to me like my father, who often criticized me. I felt like I was walking on eggs, never able to really be myself. As the seesaw of manipulation and control continued, I wondered what happened to all those dreams we had?" Vincent grows quiet and a bit withdrawn as he remembers these times.

As years went by the hurts accumulated for both of them. "It seemed to me," Vincent continues, "that she was full of so many unfounded complaints. She complained because we had only one car and she had to walk for groceries or to the doctor a few blocks away. That made me bitter because I thought that dealing with customers and their unending wishes and complaints, plus being responsible for a lot of the employees, was much harder than pushing a baby stroller to the store. She should have my job for a while!"

Vincent began to buy her things, but it seemed the more he bought her, the more she expected until "I felt like I was buying her love and affection and that made me angry.

"Our son was soon old enough to be in sports so I figured I had a legitimate reason to be away from home. I relived my own high school athletic experiences, and I had a chance to feel close to my son.

"Years passed, and our children graduated from college. We didn't have to work as hard and had more time to spend together. Yet I continued to feel that Fran didn't care much about our marriage. I also became aware that she was drinking too much, but I didn't know what to do about it. When she seemed depressed or upset, I tried to help but was unable to because she would say, 'You aren't going to tell *me* what to do'"

"If I tried being especially nice to her, it seemed to only inflame her anger and she would ask me why I hadn't done all those things before? I began to feel hopeless. I decided that she was crazy, and that *she* was the one with all the problems. When she threatened to leave I said I didn't believe her, although underneath I was afraid and unable to tell her how I felt. I even told people that she would be back, but no one knew how terrified I was that she would not," Vincent remembers.

Fran, on the other hand, busied herself compulsively with many projects to compensate for her loneliness and despair. She kept an immaculate house. "I scrubbed the walls, porches, floors *and* children in an attempt, I think, to scrub my soul clean," Fran recalls. "The more I did, the faster I spun a web around myself and the more entangled I became."

Soon there were more children and more scrubbing, more nagging Vincent to go to church, while he spent more time with sports. "I remember dressing up in a brand new green coat and a fashionable dress and a hat with a feather, all things Vincent bought for me. I went to a hockey game with him in this classy outfit, just to dress up and get out. I felt important to him that night and tried to enjoy the game. But I was still lonely and suspicious that Vincent had bought me those things to get what he wanted. The more he bought, the more I demanded and the lonelier I became. I felt like I was on a treadmill, going faster and faster until I could not get off, even if I wanted to.

"I longed to be close to Vincent, and there were times when I did try. But often he would say things like, 'You shouldn't feel that way,' or 'You *don't* feel that way,' or 'There has to be something wrong with you,' and in time I came to believe it," Fran concludes.

When the children left home for college, Fran enrolled in college herself part–time, eventually receiving a liberal arts degree. While it gave her a sense of accomplishment, it seemed to drive Vincent further away.

"I had my first drink when I was 48 years old," Fran explains. "I shall never forget the way it made me feel—relaxed and able to forget the painful void in my life. It seemed a legitimate way to escape reality and my increasing feelings of hopelessness. Slowly and insidiously I began drinking more and more, looking for reasons and creating occasions to drink.

"One day I was to take care of our granddaughter. I knew I could not drink like I now needed to and take care of this tiny child. Instead of looking forward to keeping her, I began to dread her visits. Finally this frightened me enough that I sought help, but because my father's alcoholism was considered a sin and weakness, I could hardly admit that I indeed was an alcoholic. I was overcome with guilt, fear and more loneliness, and I tried to take my life several times. When Vincent did nothing, I truly believed he no longer cared.

"I did eventually find my way to Alcoholics Anonymous where I made new friends and felt a lot of support. They seemed to really care about me, but Vincent's frequent remarks about me not being 'like *them*' reinforced my feelings of guilt and unworthiness. I came to believe he couldn't love me if he really thought I was an alcoholic," Fran says.

"I knew he was unhappy about my attending meetings, but I also knew that I needed them in order to stop drinking. I felt torn and confused again, much like I did in the tug–of–war with the children."

Vincent continued to deny that there were problems. "Under pressure he consented to accompany me to a communications seminar, but sat with his hands folded across his chest, saying, 'no problems,' with a smirk on his face. While other people laughed, I couldn't. I knew we *did* have problems, especially in communicating how we felt. I longed to do everything in my power to improve our marriage. I felt incredible frustration from his indifference and it led me to more drinking.

"The next thing I tried was a sex counselor—the only way I could get him to go for help. During one session, I remember reaching out to him and wanting to touch him and tell him how much I did care. But he resisted and said loudly and clearly, 'Fran doesn't want this marriage to work.' It was then that I truly felt hopeless.

"One anniversary evening, after we had been married for quite a few years, I told him how badly I felt and that I couldn't go on this way. His answer was typical: 'You don't really mean it.' Since I often changed my mind, he seemed to think this was just another of those times. It was as though he was just waiting to see if I was going to carry out my threat of leaving.

"The anger mounted inside me until it was like a huge pile of red hot coals in the pit of my stomach, burning out any love I had for him. I actually felt justified in leaving, since it was far better to leave than to live with someone I no longer loved. I felt as if the roomful of lights that had been my dream of our marriage and my life had gone out, one by one, and I was all alone in the dark," Fran says with profound sadness.

Vincent recalls those days somewhat differently. "At first I was glad that Fran was going to Alcoholics Anonymous, but it seemed her new friends were influencing her away from me since many of them were either separated or divorced. I did not want to believe that she might leave me. In fact, the day she started making lists of the conditions of a separation, what furniture she would take, and how much she expected in support, I just let her go, expecting that she would see things my way again. But when the moving van pulled into the drive, I was in a state of shock. I tried to hold her and tell her how much I loved her, but she was completely angry. She had her sister there to support her and help her move, and I couldn't fight them both."

Fran filed for divorce a few months after she left. Vincent made it clear through his lawyer that he wanted to reconcile, but what he received were angry letters from Fran, full of grievances of how he had hurt her, most of which he felt were unjustified.

Vincent tried to get their children to see that Fran had problems but they didn't agree, nor did they want to get involved, all of which added to Vincent's loneliness and grief.

"I would lie awake at night and review what I would do differently if I ever got a chance. I saw how my stubborn refusal to go for help and my unwillingness to admit my own failures when we did go for counseling played a large part in the breakdown of our marriage. I longed for a second chance to show her just how much I really cared. I never stopped loving her."

During their long separation, Vincent remembers how "dismal and lonely" it was to be in the house alone. "But I managed to get through it by going out with friends and becoming more involved in community and business responsibilities.

"Shortly after Fran left, a woman came into my life and showed me love and concern. I was so needy that I regretfully became more involved with her than I knew was right for me. But no matter where I went or what I did, I still longed for Fran."

Fran's experience was similar. "After we were separated for about 15 months, I met a kind, understanding man to whom I responded as a thirsty sponge does to water. In time, however, I realized that my loneliness and needs caused me to see more in the relationship than was really there.

"Sometimes people would say, 'Don't you think God could heal your marriage?' or 'I still think you two could make it.' Those thoughts stayed with me, like little seeds of hope.

"We were still separated when our youngest daughter was married. As we posed for the family picture when we really weren't a family, I felt a surge of pain and regret. Vincent showed signs of love and care for me that day when he looked at me and by the little things he said. But I refused to dance with him because I was afraid of how I would feel if he held me; he looked so handsome and appealing. I pushed aside my feelings of regret, afraid of where they might lead."

Some time later Fran went to a retreat center in Quebec to study and meditate, in an effort to refocus her life as a single woman, and to discover "God's will for my life." She did not expect, nor was she prepared, for the events that followed. "I began to see—and began to admit—my part in the demise of our marriage. One question kept following me: What would have happened if I had been different and could have seen beyond my own unmet needs? That led to more questions: Why couldn't I have understood Vincent's needs instead of blaming him for everything that was wrong? Why couldn't I accept the blame that belonged to me?

"I'll never forget one snowy day I spent in the library. I started writing down all the things I believed I had done wrong. The list was endless. I imagined, one by one, laying them down and asking for forgiveness, from God as well as from Vincent. I began to be relieved of a great burden, and a deep sense of peace and contentment slowly came over me.

"Next, I did the same things with the hurts I felt were inflicted upon me, both in childhood and in my marriage. I again asked God to help me forgive the persons who hurt me, as well as to heal the pain from those hurts. I came to understand that forgiveness is horizontal as well as vertical, and that I could be reconciled with those I felt had wronged me. I began to believe that this could happen with Vincent. The love that I had buried beneath my rubble of anger and bitterness and resentment began to flow freely through my entire being. I could hardly wait to tell Vincent.

"I decided to complete my stay at the center, using that time to think about how I needed to change. I walked and cross–country skied along beautiful water–ways and let the crisp clean air and early signs of spring speak to me of new beginnings. For the first time I felt hope!"

Meanwhile, Fran got in touch with her pastor, who then spoke with Vincent. "And I had *my* first glimmer of hope for reconciliation when her pastor told me she was at a retreat center in Quebec, making some changes in her life," Vincent recalls.

"Never will I forget the way I felt when I heard she wanted to reconcile our marriage. All I had longed for was coming true. Not only was she coming back to me, I now had another chance.

"I was afraid that after such a long separation we would both have a hard time forgiving one another for the hurts we had inflicted before and during our time apart. I had fewer fears when I read the letters from Fran's journal. There she identified many weaknesses in our marriage and said she believed we were *both* responsible, that we *both* needed to change. Hearing that, I was certainly ready to work with a counselor. I wanted to be less selfish, spend more time with her, show my love and concern for her, and generally learn how to communicate my feelings. It seemed we were finally on the right track and my hopes were high," Vincent recalls the pleasure of that anticipation.

Fran and Vincent talked with some friends who had worked diligently on their marriage and were experiencing success. The couple had gone to Recovery of Hope to facilitate that process. "We decided to try it," Vincent remembers. "So many well–meaning people were giving us so much advice, it seemed to hinder our progress. It seemed better for us to get away. Before we left, we both made a fresh commitment to our marriage and agreed to work hard on it together."

"As we drove to begin our intensive week of therapy, I felt

like I was with a stranger," Fran recalls. "We had had almost no contact with one another for two and a half years, and whatever words we had spoken were not pleasant ones. Then in the short time we were back together again, we dated, but did not live together. We needed to learn to know each other all over again.

"Hundreds of questions spun through my mind. Could we learn to trust each other again? Would we be able to break our old destructive patterns of relating? What was in store for us with counselors we didn't even know? What would they ask of us?"

Vincent and Fran worked hard during the week they were together in counseling. They looked at their families of origin, the differences in their personalities, the distinctive ways they viewed circumstances. They learned new and more satisfying ways to communicate.

"It was as though our whole lives were put on a screen and we could see how our families influenced our ways of relating to each other now. Vincent's family, for example, talked over problems and worked at solving them," Fran says. "My family argued a lot but could never settle anything.

"We looked at our pasts and relived the old hurts. As we shared them we found much healing. The counselors encouraged us to see our differences in a positive way, rather than negative. I need Vincent's quiet strength; he needs my outgoing personality. I need his ability to think things through; he needs my spontaneity.

"Restoration has not been automatic. It has not happened over night. It comes with forgiveness, with the willingness to admit when we are wrong.

"Today we try to not take each other for granted. We express appreciation, affection and affirmation whenever we can, and we look deliberately for times to do that. We also try to consider the other's needs instead of focusing on our own."

Fran continues with a vital new understanding. "I have discovered resources for help as a child of an alcoholic: books such as *Adult Children of Alcoholics* and *Codependent No More*. They have helped me understand myself and the way I relate to people, especially Vincent.

"I have also learned that the man of my dreams does not exist, that our marriage is imperfect because we are imperfect, that my happiness does not come from another person, nor does it depend on my circumstances. It comes from within me, loving and accepting myself as God loves and accepts me."

"Before we left our Recovery of Hope week to come home, we had a recommitment service, exchanged new wedding rings and looked upon our marriage as a new one."

"Our past several years together have been difficult ones. It takes time and work to let go of the past and build on the present. Because we were married for so many years, it is easy to get stuck in old patterns of relating. We have learned that continuing in counseling during those hard times is essential. We also stay in close touch with other 'recovering' couples and that has helped a lot.

"I know I'm back where I belong—with Fran," Vincent concludes.

11

Transforming Ties That Bind

"I don't know what healthy means," Ruth confessed as she sat with her husband following a session of counseling. "If I had some semblance of understanding or love or whatever it is that healthy people have, I wouldn't be in this mess. I am 40 years old and I feel wrapped in unfairness from my childhood. I am a victim of a terribly dysfunctional family," she continued, using language which had become part of her new understanding about her family of origin.

"And mine wasn't much better," Sanford adds. "When you bring the two of us together, what can you expect?"

Each could recite volumes of stories to support the belief that their experiences, many of them painful, contributed to the difficulty they were now encountering as adults in their marriage.

"I was raised in a lonely, abusive home I could barely tolerate. While my parents had problems of their own, all I knew was that I was miserable. Only a few moments of comfort from those years stand out in my mind: the bosomy, all–encompassing embrace of Mrs. Baker, my Sunday School teacher, when I was five. The soft lips of a large magnificent horse nuzzling oats from my palm—I couldn't believe he could have such large teeth and not bite me just for being little. The words of praise to God I learned in children's church choir. We were quite middle–class. To suggest we were neglected or abused would have been an outrage, so I hid it very well," Ruth remembers.

This is Sanford's story: "I was the fourth child in four years of a quickie marriage. My mother drank and my father was gone a lot. Mostly I worried about whether or not I would get enough to eat. My parents just didn't care. After I got out of high school I experimented with and abused various substances, gradually withdrawing more and more. When my mother threw me out of the house, I set out aimlessly across the country to seek fame and fortune, spending some time in ill health, and in a jail in Kentucky on false charges."

✦

"My father was an alcoholic," Roger explains. "I never knew what to expect from him. Sometimes he was very kind to me, probably trying to make up for the times when things were so ugly. Other times he turned fearsome and violent and we all knew to hide or stay out of his way. The difficult part was never knowing what to expect. I felt I could never bring friends home with me because I didn't know how he would be and I didn't want my friends to discover my situation."

✦

"My mother died unexpectedly when I was only 10 years old," Joe remembers with a residue of great sadness. "She had been the only one who seemed to truly care about me. She believed in me and encouraged me when I told her how much I wanted to be a doctor. When she died I lost all that warmth and security. I had to fend for myself and take care of my younger siblings. I can't remember much of a childhood, it was so full of responsibilities and duties. In essence I became the 'mother' of our family since Dad was away at work most of the time."

✦

The stories go on and on, each with its own poignancy, sadness and even humor, each revealing something of its teller.

Certain ones of us come from more conventional families with mothers, fathers, sisters, brothers and relatives we know—"typical families." Others of us come from "fractured" families with losses in relationships for a variety of reasons, some through no one's fault.

Our families of origin come from cities, from isolated rural areas, from tightly knit ethnic communities. One spouse may be from a large city, and quite cosmopolitan; the other may be from a small town, with little exposure beyond the state's borders. Each may be attracted to the other's uniqueness. "He grew up in Chicago and has traveled in Europe," she may say initially with pride and admiration. "She's a sweet little hometown girl," he may say, with the unspoken message being that her innocence and inexperience makes him the necessary teacher. Many times, however, what attracted the two to each other may stand formidably between them.

Others who have grown up in substantially different places may develop similar values and ideas and have overlapping experiences. These couples may defy certain odds and stay happily together.

We are all related to our families of origin in ways that we cannot always understand or recognize. We tend to recreate variations of the families from which we come, although the impact of these "ties that bind" is largely unconscious. For example, Ted says with some disbelief, "My family was never very close and I imagined that when I got married and had a family, we would do a lot of things together. I always dreamed of my wife and me planning everything together, never alone. Now I find on too many occasions, it's just easier for me to plan things without consulting my wife to find out what she wants. I've even gone on vacations alone just like Dad used to. That's something I never thought I would do.

"If you could take a picture of the inner workings of my childhood family—of my parents and brothers and sisters and what we looked like 20 years ago—and took another picture of my current family now, we probably wouldn't look all that different."

Creating the present as if it were identical to the past, sometimes with pleasure and sometimes with great chagrin, we see ourselves and our spouses and children repeating patterns of relating that we knew as youngsters.

The more we can learn and understand about our personal heritages, and the great degree to which they tend to motivate us to repeat those some behaviors and attitudes in our own families, the freer we are to *transform those ties that bind us*. We can learn to select the strengths of our families of origin and let go of their weaknesses in order to become who we really want to be in our relationships.

While it is important to know as much about our pasts as we can, the goal is otherwise—to observe ourselves and how we interact and relate *now*, and to critique and experience new ways of relating. Making our current relationships better is based both upon insights into our pasts, as well as choosing to behave toward each other differently *now*.

Be alert to one common pitfall in the process of assessing strengths and weaknesses in one's family of origin: "parent bashing," that tendency to place all responsibility for one's difficulties on the dysfunctional part of the way one was parented. Mothers have especially been blamed since they are often considered the primary caretakers or gatekeepers and are thus more responsible for the way children turn out. Mothers are criticized for either being too involved or not involved enough. They are held responsible for many difficulties that their children experience, including the more pronounced violations such as incest. They are blamed for not protecting the child and are sometimes held responsible for the father and other relatives as well

Dads, on the other hand, are often pictured as absentee parents, who, if present, are not involved enough with child care. As a society we hold confusing—often constricting—definitions of their roles.

One mother asked recently, rather wearily, as she listened to a lengthy discourse on dysfunctional families, "Are there ever any functional families?" The question is valid.

There are, without debate, many persons who have been deeply damaged, who have been robbed of their right to a "normal" childhood because of neglect, abuse and physical or mental violence experienced at the hands of those who should have been their caretakers. Many of these people continue to suffer enormously as adults. They learned early on to protect themselves from thinking, feeling and sensing, but not addressing, what was real. Through it all they lost their ability to trust themselves and others. Many come to believe that they are bad, that they should not have needs, that they are at fault, somehow unworthy and unentitled. Added to that are their families' insistence on blind loyalty. That demand comes so that the abuse can continue without "dissent or disagreement" of any kind (Calof: 2).

Adult survivors of incest and child abuse require careful, particular and sensitive help, usually over a long period of time. There are those who are unable to remember or talk about the profound pain they have experienced. Only with great difficulty, the assistance of highly sensitive experts and hard work are they able to recall and talk about these extremely damaging events, and finally move toward healing.

People have a right to be angry for the deep hurts they experienced as children. They need to express those feelings, although not always directly to their parents. It is often more helpful to deal with the effects of such events in safe settings with caring, professional people.

Parents tend to believe that they will not repeat what was painful for themselves with their own children. Without thought and conscious decisions to change, however, they may find themselves parenting in those same ways. Their children, then, become parents who also have a difficult time parenting, and the cycle seems to go on and on. Retaliation and blame keep emerging.

Examining the outrageous, harmful pain and the nearly forgotten fears that find their ways into our adult lives is a long and often arduous journey. None of us have chosen our parents or our experiences. What happened to us as children is not our fault. But as adults, we no longer need to be victims. We can learn self-parenting skills which are loving and nurturing, becoming "our own good parent," in order to become better parents to our own children.

As we journey toward greater self–understanding we can

choose to understand our parents' lives, thus opening a new kind of relationship with them; one that *transforms* "the ties that bind." The process can honor both generations, ours and our parents, acknowledging their hurts as well as ours.

Parents, despite their best intentions, cannot always understand their children. Furthermore, they, too, have been strongly influenced by their own parents who grew up in a still different generation with its particular expectations of mothers, fathers and children. While some parents have wilfully abused their children, it is not as though parents know all the right things to do and choose not to act appropriately. Sam's story (Chapter 7) illustrates this clearly. He had always wondered about his family, especially his mother: "I was given to my aunt and uncle to raise and knew almost nothing about my mother's life as a child, except that she had lived in a children's home. I did not know what became of her family or who they were. I often wondered why she left my sisters and me.

"Recently, when Marie and I were telling our story at a church, we met someone who knew my family and had some information about my mother! I learned that in her early childhood, she lived in a foster home and spent her teenage years in a children's home. I wondered why she was placed there.

"Then around the time she was 16, her mother (my grandmother) hired two gunmen in a plot to kidnap her from the home," Sam goes on, amazement still apparent in his voice.

Tantalized by his own unfolding story, Sam went to the local library and found the newspaper with the account of the kidnapping. "A mixture of feelings washed over me as I read the front page headlines, saw pictures of my mother and read the account of the story about my *own* family. It told about my grandparents, aunts and uncles, stories I had never heard before."

Most of what Sam learned was "not very good." With more research he learned that his mother's father was abusive. "That's probably why she was taken away from her parents," he continues. "She married my father completely against his parents' wishes. I can remember my grandfather saying to my father, 'You and the children can come home but not *her*.'

"So my mother, too, must have felt rejection all her life, just as

I did. I find it easier to understand and forgive her now that I know more about what her life was like." Sam has a further regret. "I wish only that she were still living so I could tell her this."

Sam has done more to make peace with his parents. His efforts have been vital to his own healing, as well as his relationship with Marie. "My father lives in another state and I rarely see him. But recently when I visited him, I told him that I wanted him to know I forgave him for having left our family. I wanted him to know that I really cared about him. I told him about my sadness and grief that I didn't really know him, that we didn't have father–son times together.

"Although he gave me little response—and I understand that—I feel good about letting him know I forgive him," Sam concludes.

Many movements, groups, therapies, books and people are giving themselves, often quite effectively, to bringing healing and restoration to adult children who have experienced devastating events and relationships in their families or with close relatives. It is empowering to learn that you are not alone in these painful experiences, that others have similar injuries in their pasts. To talk about these powerful secrets which have been stuffed inside for years is an experience of release.

Many church and faith communities have all too often been part of a continuing system of denial, instead of offering validation and the freedom for persons to tell their stories, thereby finding acceptance and entitlement. A stance of judgment and blame only makes the pain more poignant and difficult for both parents and children who tend to blame themselves already or who see themselves as victims.

Blame, from whatever quarters, is, in the end, defeating and life–absorbing. Continuing to blame our parents, for example, does not bring healing. While it may work for a while as we try to resolve our problems, blame usually leads to continuing unsatisfactory relationships.

Anger and denial must first be acknowledged and lived through. That is the first step, and likely the most difficult one. But it does not constitute healing. It may involve facing those choices we made personally that now stand in the way of building satisfying relationships. It may mean granting that our parents made some poor choices. It may also illumine how we parent our own children.

The road to wholeness and becoming unstuck ultimately includes forgiveness. This is not a glossed–over denial of the profound pain and sadness we have experienced. It is, instead, a way of actively dealing with issues, of eventually letting go of judging others. Forgiveness can free any of us from powerful ties that bind and constrict us, and can help us emerge from our past to negotiate new kinds of relationships of our own choosing. We can choose not to be victims any longer.

There are those rare persons who can forgive "once and done," as in the case of Martin and Sue (Chapter 14). More often forgiveness is a process, and usually a most difficult one, that begins with an urge to move on from the hurts we have experienced. The process tends to go slowly as we deal, sometimes piece by piece, with the pain and hurt we have known.

One victim struggling to rise above his injury told those who had wronged him, "You violated my trust and now you ask me to forgive you. I do. But trust and respect is something you earn. I need time to feel you have earned that right. I want that to happen, but it will take time."

Even when we believe we have forgiven, those wrongs and painful events will always be part of our history, continuing to surface throughout our lives, sometimes when we least expect them. In those moments, however difficult, we can choose to forgive again. In that way we are in charge of how we will feel and what we will do. We need no longer be victims of our past. The power of the people and events who earlier violated us need not continue to be restricting and confining. We are free to move on from those ties that bind.

Dwight Lee Wolter writes in *Forgiving our Parents* that the question is no longer: "Who is to blame?" or "How could they have done those things?" Instead, the question is: "Who has been hurt and how can we get him/her back on track?" He concludes: "As we begin to forgive our parents, we begin to forgive ourselves. And we begin to forgive the world for not being perfect either."

Transforming the ties that bind us is a way to continue becoming all we are meant to be.

12

But We're Such Nice People

Jeff is an up–and–coming bank manager; Shelly has a business of her own. Together they have two children. The setting—one would think—for an ideal marriage.

"In our early years we rarely fought, we were best friends, we enjoyed doing things together. We made a good team," Shelly reflects. "We were committed to our marriage, but sometimes I felt more like we were roommates. The intimacy and closeness I had idealistically hoped for just wasn't there. I often said we could talk about anything, but I could never talk about my many unmet expectations or my feelings of inadequacy. I just assumed that I wasn't a good enough wife or that he wasn't able to be the husband I wanted. And on we went with life."

Jeff describes what he brought into the marriage. "I grew up in a calm and stable environment whose guiding philosophy was 'peace at any price.' I learned never to argue, never to get angry—and to swallow my hurts and frustrations. We neither showed or shared emotions. We rarely shouted; we also rarely laughed. Whenever my father gets a little boisterous even now, my mother reins him in with 'Oh, Robert...' Through example and discussion, I became self–effacing, self–sacrificing and non-assertive.

"My parents passed on a pile of *oughts* and *shoulds* to guide my life. Sometimes that pile still overwhelms me. On top of that, my mother's method of discipline was the 'Guilt Trip.' She worked hard to be sure I behaved 'properly,' while my father sat in silent judgment, manipulating my behavior through stories, never owning his feelings, but passing them off as belonging to others. He used guilt, withholding of approval, and uncertainty to bring about the behavior he desired, and I anxiously responded.

"My mother ran our house. She is a hardworking lady with a keen sense of duty and doing the 'right thing,' which includes *always* putting others first. In our household no one, especially not me, had to make choices. We weren't even asked what we wanted to drink with a meal, it was just there."

Jeff remembers that his father spent most of his time working. Having lived through the Depression he was determined to give his family economic security. The man had been taught that one's self–worth depended on working hard. He viewed anyone who failed to meet that standard of total dedication to work as lazy and undeserving.

"I didn't see much of my father as I grew up, except at dinner," Jeff says. "If he talked at all, it was lectures. He seemed to expect everyone to anticipate or guess his needs.

"My parents' marriage seemed solid enough, but I believe they simply accepted what was. They swallowed their feelings instead of discussing them. Not surprisingly, they showed each other little overt affection. I didn't feel free to enjoy life until I moved out of my parents' home and went away to college. It was during those years I met Shelly," Jeff says with a grin.

"I saw her first at a New Year's Eve party. She and her date had arrived late and she made an elegant entry! I can still remember what she wore. A year later we were both without dates on New Year's Eve and friends set us up as a blind date. That was the beginning."

Since they were attending different colleges, their relationship was often long–distance. They had fun and turmoil. "Many dates ended with Shelly in tearful confusion," explains Jeff. "Sometimes it concerned me; other times it frustrated me. I remember thinking if I would just stand by—be there—that we would come out of it together."

As one might expect from his orderly organized background, Jeff had their future planned. They would get married, both work a year and save some money. Then after another year, "to get used to being married," he would go to graduate school. Children, he thought, would have to wait.

"Our wedding day came. I was proud to be marrying Shelly. As I waited in the church with my best man, the photographer asked if I was nervous. I wasn't nervous. Everything was going according to plan. One week after our honeymoon, I went back to my second year at the bank—with a promotion!"

Shelly remembers anticipating a new life. "I couldn't wait to get married. I was anxious to get out of my parents' home where I never felt much love. In fact, I felt more like a burden, like I was too much trouble. I was the fourth child and the youngest in the family. I often wondered if I was adopted, there were so few pictures of me and hardly anything filled out in my baby book."

Shelly felt like she was never old enough to do what her big brothers and sisters could do, or that she was the unwanted tag–along. She felt that what she liked or wanted was never considered and that she was always too young to have her opinions taken seriously.

"I figured that if I would just be happy all the time I wouldn't be a bother and everything would okay. But I couldn't *always* be happy and, when I wasn't, I would become depressed thinking how awful I was to be around, how I was making everyone else miserable, and I would pout. My parents would taunt me, 'Poor little old Shelly,' and I would become sadder still.

"If I were to draw a picture of my family, everyone but me would be on the inside of a circle. I would be on the outside, alone and unable to get in. I tried so hard to please my parents in lots of ways. I was in the advanced sections in school, but they said I never worked up to my potential. I could never be good enough.

"My mother even wondered if I was good enough for Jeff, and when Jeff talked to my father about marrying me, he warned Jeff about how moody I was."

Shelly's father always had the right opinion. If her mother expressed an idea contrary to his, he angrily put her down. There was no give–and–take. "I can actually picture my mother stuffing words back into her mouth, words that had caused my father to yell at her.

"That would certainly never happen to me, not with Jeff as my husband. He didn't get angry. He always asked what I wanted to do and was anxious to please me. My opinions were important to him. He wanted to be with me and loved me, moods and all. We could talk about anything. Life with him would be truly special. I would be loved. I would be inside that family circle with him."

After a "wonderful honeymoon," Jeff and Shelly settled into their apartment and Jeff started back to work. And their lives began to revolve around his work. "We couldn't go out during the week, even for shopping, because he had brought some papers home from the bank to work on," Shelly says. "If we went away on weekends, we had to get home early on Sunday so he could prepare for work and study for a course he was taking that would mean a promotion." Shelly began to feel that she was competing with his work and anything else he had to do. She came last.

"I expected Jeff's sexual interest in me to continue after we were married. Our honeymoon validated my expectations—we were almost like the cartoons, with newspapers piling up outside the hotel room door. But after that, things changed. Sex became a last priority. Jeff took his books to bed instead of me, his new wife!" Shelly says with some indignation. "I decided there must be something wrong with me. I wasn't interesting enough or good enough in bed to take him away from his books."

She acknowledges that Jeff was quite agreeable though. "It seemed as if my desire was his desire. 'What do you want for dinner, hon?' I'd ask. 'Oh, whatever you'd like to make,' he would answer. 'What do you want to do tonight?' 'Oh, whatever you want.' Sometimes I pressed him: 'I'd really like to know what you want to do once in a while.' And he would respond, 'What I want to do is what *you* want to do. Is there anything wrong with that?'

"It just didn't seem natural to me that he could *always* want what I wanted, but who could condemn that kind of devotion?" Shelly questions.

"Over the years though," Shelly continues, "I began to see his agreeability as his way of avoiding making a decision. It was easier for me to choose for him. I felt like most of the decisions rested on my shoulders. He even asked me what I thought he should wear, or whether a shirt was clean enough to wear another day! I began to feel as though I was his boss or mother, not his wife and lover. And since he never said what he wanted, I had to guess at what would please him, hoping I guessed right."

Shelly remembers that when they had a disagreement, which rarely happened, she would continue stating her case until Jeff eventually conceded that she was right, ending with, "Whatever you say." Somehow it didn't feel right to her. Either she was bullying him, or he was holding his private, different opinion and just giving in to placate her.

Jeff neither criticized Shelly, nor complimented her. She concluded that she was not measuring up to his standards. "I might try a new recipe that I thought turned out great, and he would say, 'You know, this would really be good if you put tomato sauce and mozzarella on it.' Or if I asked how I looked, he would find a little something to fix up."

The problems that troubled them in the early part of their marriage continued to disturb them—sex, decision-making, Jeff's need to please, Shelly's need for affirmation, and friction over the amount of time Jeff's job took.

Jeff reflects on those early years. "Shelly wanted to make love many evenings during the week. I had just started a new job with more responsibilities and I felt compelled to prepare at home in order to continue my move up in the bank. One *must* work before playing. So weekends became the time for intimacy. But things didn't go well sexually. Both of us felt like failures. So we tried seeing a therapist. Unfortunately, his suggestion—have a drink and take a vacation—was so superficial that sex remained an uncomfortable and unresolved issue."

Jeff didn't understand why saying, "Do whatever you want" was so frustrating to Shelly. "I only wanted to please her, but it was obvious that I didn't. What *did* she want?"

Jeff completed graduate school, Shelly finished college with honors and landed a rewarding job. They settled into a comfortable lifestyle in a split–level suburban home.

"But our approaches to our problems remained the same. Shelly would go into blue funk and I would be silently resentful, each of us waiting for the other to make a move," Jeff recalls. "I *always* assumed that what was upsetting Shelly involved me. Since she said nothing to change my assumption, I would withdraw, avoiding conflict.

"To try to make her happy I would go on a binge of doing things around the house. But that only seemed to create more conflict. I was completely frustrated! I was doing all I could and nothing helped. Me, do anything wrong? Never! I was such a nice guy. I just kept burying the problems and feelings—it was the only way I knew how to deal with them—and carrying a vague ache that things weren't what they could be."

Despite all that, Shelly and Jeff agree that during this time they always liked each other, respected each other's capabilities and were a good team, with real trust in each other's faithfulness.

After 11 years of personal satisfaction in their work and careers, Jeff and Shelly decided to have children. Little did they realize what stress that would cause in their relationship! Their first child arrived, bringing all their buried problems to the surface with a vengeance.

Shelly's rather conservative employer made it impossible for her to return to her job. She lost the outside stimulus and affirmation which had been so much a part of her life.

"Shelly had always fought low self-esteem. Staying home day after day aggravated that and further undermined our intimacy and sexual relations. The demands of child care left her drained. She would say to me, 'Don't touch me!' seeing any physical contact as another demand. That rejection really hurt me. I wanted to help and comfort her, but neither one of us had much emotional energy to give."

Shelly became quite depressed after the birth of their child. The stress increased. "We were surviving," Jeff says. "We performed for parents and friends. I didn't know what to expect each night when I came home. Sometimes Shelly saw my work as competition; other times she saw it as an unfair break from the baby that she couldn't get. She thrust the baby on me the minute I stepped through the door. She seemed to set up situations that forced me to make choices between home and work. I responded predictably—with my usual, angry withdrawal. Why did she *do* this? I remember walking one night and thinking, if we can just get through this, we'll never have another child. Everything seemed to be falling apart. I was frightened. I prayed that nothing terrible would happen," Jeff remembers clearly.

Shelly tells about this period of time as she remembers it. "I was almost 31 and it was time to have a child—now or never. Since I wanted to breastfeed my baby I didn't see how to balance the demands of this new family situation with those of my job, which included frequent overnight travel and a short maternity leave. I decided it would be best if I focused on being a Mom.

"After the birth of our child, life changed—a lot! I no longer had a stimulating, financially rewarding job. I was stuck at home taking care of a demanding infant with no family or friends around for support. I felt totally alone. The big events of the day were Jeff's going to and coming home from work. I looked to him for everything, especially to relieve me of the constant demands of mothering. My world grew smaller. I gained weight. I was boring. I hated my life.

"I wondered if Jeff loved me at all. He probably just stayed with me out of duty. He was such a nice guy; he deserved someone better than me, someone who would appreciate all he did. My mother had been right, Jeff was too good for me. I had come to believe I was on the outside of *Jeff's* circle and couldn't get in.

"Just before our daughter was two, I hit the depths of depression. No one loved me but the baby, who knew no better and who deserved a better mother. My only value was as a maid and babysitter and Jeff could hire someone to do those things better than I. Then he would not have to be burdened with a moody, nagging wife. Everyone would be better off without me.

"On the way to visit my parents one day, I sat in the back seat behind Jeff and planned to jump out of the car into oncoming traffic. I didn't do it, but I was scared. Was there no escape for me?" Shelly remembers the pain of that penetrating question.

When Shelly sought individual therapy, hope returned. Jeff went with her and together they seemed to be making good progress. They decided to have a second child, but then some familiar responses began to emerge. Shelly thought Jeff wasn't involved enough in the childbirth classes; she didn't feel close to him. "It seemed sometimes that he forgot I was pregnant. I wanted special attention, but he focused more and more on work."

Shelly's depression returned. This time counseling made little difference. She believed her therapist and Jeff were ganging up on her. It seemed they thought the problems were all *her* fault. "Jeff was perfect! If I could just pull myself together, everything would be okay—the same old feelings I had with my family as a child.

"But I knew Jeff wasn't perfect. I could fill a page with things he could fix up!" she says emphatically. "It wasn't fair that I had to do all the changing. Couldn't Jeff see how badly I was hurting? Couldn't he see what he had to do to make me happy? I concluded that I wasn't worth noticing, that Jeff didn't care how I felt, that things would never change."

Some vital understanding, however, had taken root within Shelly. "I began to learn that it is important for me to love, care for and value myself. That surprised me. All my life my mother had warned me that I shouldn't think too highly of myself. That had clearly put loving myself out of the question.

"Somehow I developed the notion that I could only deserve love if I were perfect, and I knew I wasn't perfect. If I were perfect I would be able to satisfy Jeff's and the children's needs— all with ease and a smile. If I were perfect my needs would be satisfied taking care of my family and home. If I were perfect I would....and the list went on. To me perfection equalled worthiness, lovability and happiness. So I worked and worked at learning to love me and accept myself with my imperfections— to become a completed circle on my own—and I made progress," Shelly says with satisfaction.

Jeff and Shelly eventually decided to undertake a week of intensive marital therapy. Jeff recalls some of his seesawing emotions about the decision. "I confess to dreading a whole week with just my wife—maybe it will be a breakthrough. I don't want months of discussion; I want to solve the problem now. I know we need to work on our marriage together. Shelly can't fix it by herself. I have a role to play if our marriage is to get better."

The week shed light on how differently they approached things. Shelly tends to be practical, Jeff creative. Shelly likes to have things pinned down, Jeff's real nature (despite the influence of his home) is to be flexible. They looked at their families and how those roles and feelings they formed there were brought into their marriage.

Shelly says, "Those feelings of inadequacy and unimportance I had as I was growing up came right along with me, and I interpreted Jeff's behavior based on those assumptions. I learned that Jeff's putting work first and our relationship last was a result of his demanding work–ethic upbringing, not because I wasn't good enough.

"We discovered that my tendency to dominate and Jeff's willingness to let me was also part of what I had experienced at home. My father ruled everything and I wanted to avoid bringing that along with me. I didn't want to be the boss, but Jeff was comfortable with my dominance because his mother ran their family.

"Through psychodrama I actually experienced how strongly I resisted accepting and loving myself. Learning to totally accept, care for and love myself will probably be a life–long task for me. I am uncomfortable saying 'Shelly, I love you, you're a good person,' out loud. I almost can't say it now," Shelly looks a bit embarrassed. "Somehow it sounds conceited.

"I had expected to be able to accept Jeff's love for me, even though I didn't love me. But no matter what he said or did, I discounted it. If he said, 'I love to hug you,' I would think, 'Too bad he has so much to hug,' or 'He just wants to get me in bed.'

"As I've accepted myself, I am also becoming less judgmental of Jeff. Those little things he does that drive me crazy are the same little things that make him the special person he is!" she grins.

Shelly has made a conscious effort to develop a network of

friends. She joined a cooperative nursery school when her children were young, where she met with other women and children. She became more active in their church and community organizations. This helped relieve Jeff of the tremendous burden of providing her only adult companionship.

"About a year ago I took another step in accepting myself," Shelly says. "I joined Overeaters Anonymous. I realized that, like an alcoholic or drug addict, I no longer had control over food. It controlled me. I was obsessed about my weight and food. Through the Twelve Step program of O.A. I have come to understand that I am a compulsive overeater. I'm learning what I have to do to keep my sanity around food. This program has brought me an inner peace I had only hoped existed."

Jeff continues, "I came to realize that my family's emphasis on 'peace at any price' was unnatural. It caused me to bury emotions. Feelings and emotions aren't a smorgasbord where I can pick and choose; I have to take everything or nothing.

"I began to see some sides of me from Shelly's viewpoint. I realized that my withdrawal from conflict was accompanied by a quiet, smug, judgmental attitude. On the outside I was that 'nice guy,' but inside burned frustration, anger, resentment and judgment. In fact, I am learning to allow myself to feel anger and communicate it. My 'nice guy' behavior only fed a cycle that caused minor problems and situations to spiral downward, widening the communication gap.

"I can't change Shelly, only the way I respond to her. I still hurt if she rejects my love, but rather than withdrawing, I try to remember these are the times when she needs my support the most. She may be feeling unworthy or inadequate and that needs to be dealt with right away," Jeff emphasizes.

With a smile, he continues, "Our new communication has enhanced our sex life. We ask for and tell each other what we want and need without trying to guess. We believe that each wants to please the other."

There is a new piece to this puzzle. Shelly has recently, with the careful guidance and assistance of professionals, begun to have memories of being sexually abused by her father when she was quite young. "I can hardly express how painful this is," she says with great sadness. "But in the pain I am finding a new understanding of myself. No wonder I never felt my parents loved me, no wonder I felt on the outside, no wonder I chose a husband who would not overpower me, no wonder sex has been a problem for me and Jeff. This underscores the idea that our marital difficulties are more a symptom of unresolved individual issues than being the primary problem," Shelly concludes.

"Our marriage is a joyful struggle," Jeff says describing their journey together. "We need to sort out what we want to keep from our families and what is causing conflict and needs to be discarded."

"Sometimes I ask Jeff why something so good has to be so hard?" Shelly smiles. "We are in an on–going process of learning and changing. We will never relate perfectly. When we go through rough times it's easy to revert to our old ways. But we have learned how to step back and re–evaluate before making negative judgments about ourselves or each other. We can forgive ourselves for making mistakes and go on from there. We have some new skills to work with. Instead of trying to change each other, we are making an effort to appreciate the special qualities we each bring to our marriage. Our individual circles are becoming complete and they connect in love."

13

Systems and Themes: Pursuer-Distancer

Another theme that characterizes many marriages, is the "pursuer-distancer" relationship. This surfaces when one spouse pursues the other in an attempt to become close, while the other spends energy distancing and resisting the intimacy. Change comes when one spouse finds the roles unacceptable and attempts to get unstuck, causing imbalance, a signal for change.

The person who wants most to have the relationship work, who expends the greatest energy and effort to bring about change, has the least power to make it happen. The person who cares the least has the most power in the relationship. Indifference, or not caring--refusing to try to make things work--is a powerful position.

Usually the person with the most power has the lesser need for intimacy and closeness. Distance and indifference are most frustrating to the person who wants to change.

George and Dawn lived in Indonesia, where he was employed by a large international banking firm.

"As part of my work, I was always busy with people and developed several close friendships. Increasingly I found it easier to spend time with them than with Dawn. I involved her less and less in the 'important' parts of my life and we slowly became more and more distant. Dawn began complaining about my coldness toward her. I refused to admit anything was wrong and, in turn, became very critical of her," George explains.

"George, I have a sitter for the baby tonight. I made reservations for dinner and reserved tickets to hear the City Center concert," Dawn called at work to tell George. The gesture was uncharacteristic of her. He was the one who usually engineered such events. Dawn, sensing acutely that things were not as they should be, decided to be more assertive and made plans herself for just the two of them.

George also responded uncharacteristically, criticizing her for not checking with him first. "We can't afford the luxury of an evening like this. If you'd pay more attention to the checkbook, you'd know that," he snapped over the phone. "I have plans tonight anyway and can't cancel them without warning."

Dawn remembers how his response confused her. "I knew our relationship was changing drastically, but I couldn't put my finger on the specific cause. I didn't know how to react to it. I felt as if I were riding a roller coaster; some days depressed about our relationship, other days determined to change myself. Sometimes I did everything I could to please him; the next day I nagged at him about everything I found disagreeable. Rejections like the one about an evening out together made me feel so distant from him. When I talked to him about it he said I was imagining things and dismissed it."

Dawn describes George as the one who did most of the talking in their relationship. "He drew out my thoughts and feelings when I tended to suppress them. He tried to help me find workable solutions to problems I was facing. When there was friction between us he was the one who responded openly and honestly."

Now it had all changed. Dawn tried to encourage him to talk with her, and other times demanded that he communicate telling him it was his responsibility. "He stopped initiating any conversation between us and acted very put off, even apathetic, when I tried to talk about anything. I felt alone as I never had before. Here we were, in our second year of a three year contract. We had just entered our second foreign country, and I had no friends. George had been my friend. I depended on him. And so I clung to him more and more, and he withdrew from me accordingly. I was deeply hurt by it all, often crying myself to sleep."

Dawn began to feel ugly and insecure. She started talking to her own image in the mirror, trying to convince herself that she *was* good and beautiful, that God did still love her.

Not only was there no one to support her, she felt George becoming increasingly critical of everything she did, especially her mothering. In a sense, as Dawn became more and more self–critical, she was giving George permission to further critique her and create more distance between them. Becoming pregnant only deepened her lethargy and lack of energy.

"I refused to admit that anything was wrong and I began to resent her rather obvious attempts to recover intimacy," George acknowledges. "I felt trapped and claustrophobic, as if she was trying to hold me down, and I reacted by pulling away even more. This led to a nearly complete isolation between us, and I began to think we were doomed to a failed relationship. I felt extremely guilty about ruining our marriage and yet oddly apathetic about the whole thing, assuming it was inevitable that a bad marriage would break up." There was nothing to do to make any difference, he concluded, and the consequences didn't matter. The dissonance in his mind, however, became more and more difficult for him to handle. He became physically ill and lost about 25 pounds.

"One night I went to the local bar, sat in the disco and got drunk. Late that night Dawn came looking for me, finally found me and wanted to know if I was all right. She wanted to take me home, but I refused to go with her. I chose to stay with others whom I felt appreciated me more, and I can remember saying to them after she left, 'Oh, good, she's gone,' over and over again."

George continued to block Dawn out of his life, burying himself in business, sports and bars to try to escape the "ugliness of being at home and having to deal with the situation in which I found myself."

Subsequently, George explains, "I developed an infatuation with a woman, which started innocently enough. I visited her several times in the town where she lived and we stayed in close contact with letters and phone calls." Not only was George creating space for himself, this new relationship allowed him to again be the pursuer, with no strings attached. Dawn, on the other hand, found herself in the role of pursuer–investigator.

"I followed up on some of George's stories about where he had been and confronted him with facts he couldn't deny. I didn't want to believe he was lying to me. He had never done that to me before. But it was as though he couldn't stop seeing her. He told me about a time he had spent with her and asked my forgiveness. I thought it was over between them, but I underestimated the depth of the relationship."

George recalls his torment, "When Dawn caught me in the act of arranging another meeting, my world suddenly came crashing down around me. All hope was gone; I knew I had blown everything. I was unable to face reality and tried to run away to a small offshore island. There I wouldn't have to face anyone I knew."

Dawn called the personnel liaison at the bank to tell them she was leaving the country and to request their assistance in arranging her travel. Relieved in a certain way that she now understood better what was contributing to the "rift" between them, she knew she could no longer stay with him. She also realized how much she needed her family and friends at home to help her sort out her life.

"At that point, I took no thought of George and his feelings because I didn't think I could trust him anyway," Dawn says. "He must have felt pinned down or smothered because he left without telling anyone where he was going. I continued for the next week to make plans to leave."

Dawn tried to prepare herself mentally for what she was about to do: fly home with their little daughter to start an entirely different life. "I was so proud and convinced that I could work this out by myself. But it was like trying to sew a patch on a leaky balloon with a needle and thread!"

Just before she was scheduled to leave, George phoned her and asked, "Are you still getting ready to leave? You haven't changed your mind?"

"I couldn't believe what I was hearing," Dawn recalls. "I told him we were scheduled to leave immediately—and then he said he wanted to come too!"

George continues, "I began to realize that I wanted my marriage to Dawn to work and that it was worth any amount of effort that would make it right. But after I decided that, I had to contact Dawn to see if she even wanted me and would let me accompany her back home. I was extremely afraid that I had gone too far and that she would want no part of me. So with a great fear of rejection I begged her forgiveness and asked permission to return.

"Fortunately, God blessed me with a wife who has an incredible capacity for forgiveness. She told me she wanted us to go home together and make our marriage work. I was overwhelmed with relief and hope. I knew I would have to earn Dawn's love and trust again. At the same time we committed ourselves to each other and to get help and remain together."

Working out the mechanics for their trip home was only the first of many awkward occasions. They were apprehensive about their time together on the flight; they dreaded facing their families, although both knew that home was where they wanted to be. "We spent the long flight home quite pensively and nervously," they remember.

George reflects on his great sense of relief when he no longer needed to hide his behavior from Dawn. "We had been living double lives," George says (A common practice couples devise to prevent their "systems" from becoming imbalanced). "In the hidden part of this double life we were falling to pieces; in the public part we put on an 'everything is great, how can we help you' life. To my great shame we now had to expose the secret we had not wanted anyone to know." Both George and Dawn had received the same message from their families of origin: hide the truth if you are disappointed with life or if you are not living according to the moral rules you were taught.

George remembers his struggle to ask for help. "I didn't want to be seen as a failure at home. I was the proud carrier of our family's theme--if you're really strong, you should be able to handle things by yourselves."

Dawn's personal hurdle was similar. "Before our trouble began, I leaned on George for almost everything: to get me to talk, to help me make decisions, to set my life and spiritual goals. I've learned through this process of reconciliation to be more responsible for my decisions, thoughts and actions, for developing my own spiritual goals and ideas. Although our families were shocked, they helped in the best way they could. They showed George and me that we were still part of them, and that they loved and accepted us, something we both needed so much."

"I've learned," says George, "that love depends on commitment and not on feelings and situations. We act lovingly toward each other out of simple obedience to God and to our marriage commitment. Even if I feel apathetic or uncaring, I can still treat her in a loving way.

"I also decided that she will be my friend, and I will make her an important part of my life. We spend more time together, we talk about our experiences and feelings. We depend on each other in a healthy way now. We date each other no matter how busy we are! That means we get a babystitter and go out just to talk and visit and stay in touch with each other on a regular basis." George states this with conviction.

"I needed to learn to love George all over again in order to establish a healthy, growing relationship," Dawn adds. "I did that slowly. Love didn't come like it first did years before. Then I was head over heels in love with infatuation. Now I consciously decide to love and trust George. I bring to my mind earlier romantic episodes with him. I imagine them happening again, in a new setting. And I have stopped simply responding to what he says or does. While I take responsibility for my own attitudes and actions, it isn't always easy to do. Changing old patterns and ways of responding is hard."

Dawn and George can chart their earlier patterns of relating: distancing and pursuing, acting out themes and messages from their families of origin. Sensitive therapy brought them to understand how and why they related to each other as they did. Hard work, forgiveness and continued counseling have given them new ways of relating that bring both of them satisfaction.

14

Survivors

"When my father died of cancer 21 years ago, I thought that all my past dealings with his alcoholism were over. Wrong! Living with an alcoholic has affected my entire life. I read everything I can get my hands on about adult children of alcoholics. I meet with a support group because we have a lot of the same feelings. We laugh and cry together; we are growing and recovering together.

"But the real beginning of my healing process was going to my father's grave to talk to him," Rachel explains emphatically. "I told him how sorry I was that he had such an unhappy life, that I understood why he had turned to alcohol. But I also told him how that had affected me, and that I needed to be released from that life so that I could be free to love my husband the way I wanted. I could no longer carry the pain and guilt I had always felt.

"My father was born in South America, a child of missionaries. They died when he and his twin brother were only six months old. These little babies were returned to the States where they were raised in an obligatory way by stern and strict relatives who were unable to show them much love."

Rachel's mother was one of eight children born to a poor day laborer and his wife. The children were hired out at ages eight and nine, and were expected to work at difficult tasks, turning the money they made over to their parents. They were able to complete only grade school.

"After my parents were married, my father became a potato farmer in Idaho on a grand scale, raising over 100 acres of potatoes each summer. My mother didn't work outside our home when I was small." When Rachel was four years old, they moved into a beautiful new home in a rural area, with not many children in the neighborhood. "I remember being very lonely," Rachel recalls. "I was the only child until my sister came along when I was seven." Soon after we moved into that home, my father began drinking excessively, first wine and then whiskey. I saw a lot of bottles under the cellar steps—that's where he drank.

"During my childhood and teen years, he was sick a lot—in and out of the hospital with G.I. bleeding and cirrhosis. He would go to Alcoholics Anonymous for a while, but he always went back to drinking. I worried about him, wondering what would happen next. He was never physically abusive. He just sat quietly in his easy chair, not talking about anything. Sometimes I thought he was in a stupor.

"Mother was a mild, passive individual who wouldn't leave him because she couldn't support herself and us. She believed she was married for better or for worse. I knew my parents loved me, even though they never told me.

"When I was a freshman in high school, we lost our beautiful home because of my father's drinking and some bad investments. During the next several years we moved five times, which meant I had to constantly change schools. For me that was the end of the world!

"My father continued to drink. One time he had d.t.'s and a friend had to come to stay with us. For several days and nights he didn't sleep. He hallucinated and it scared me terribly! I went to stay with an aunt and uncle for a few days after that, much to my relief. I always enjoyed their home because we had fun there and I could go to the movies, which I wasn't allowed to do at home."

Rachel attended a conservative church with her mother. "I was terrified of their 'fire and brimstone' revival meetings," she recalls, "and I actually became physically ill when I was made to go there. I came to believe that God was angry, and that no matter how good I was, I would never be good enough to go to heaven.

"When I was a senior in high school, I won a scholarship to enter nursing school. It was a dream come true. I entered the Pocatello School of Nursing and loved being away from home. I still worried about my parents, even though I was removed from the turmoil there.

"I did well in school and enjoyed the social life that went with it. During that time my father was admitted to the hospital with d.t.'s again, and, much to my shame, some of my classmates had to take care of him. Another time he didn't pay my tuition and again I was ashamed.

"I had a lot of boyfriends as I think back. I must have been looking for some kind of acceptance and security. Things would always start out well, but then I would become so intent on making the relationship work that I would scare the guy off and would end up hurt, time after time.

"I met Mike on a blind date. We were introduced by mutual friends, and we dated steadily for about nine months. Then I became involved with someone else and ended up going from one relationship to another. At the close of my senior year, I thought about Mike again and decided to see if he would go with me to a school dance. I knew he hadn't dated anyone for the two years while I had been off and running. There was something about him I couldn't forget.

"We became quite serious. He was everything I wanted in a husband—kind, considerate, loving and the kind of man who would be a good father. And, he didn't smoke or drink. His not drinking was very important to me."

At the end of the summer, Mike left for the Navy. Rachel missed him "terribly," and they wrote to each other every day. His Thanksgiving letter to Rachel was a proposal for marriage. The wedding happened at Christmas when he was home on leave, a beautiful time they both remember happily.

Mike settles back in his chair as he begins his story. "My mother came from a large Catholic family of 18 children. Because they were quite poor she had to drop out of school after the eighth grade and get a job. She was married at 18 and had my sister when she was 19 and me when she was 20. She was pregnant when they married, but to this day no one has ever mentioned it in our family.

"Every Sunday afternoon when I was a kid, we went to Butler to my Catholic grandmother's house. I loved it there! Nobody held anything back. They hugged each other, they argued, they laughed, they drank and they had fun. They were there for each other if there was a tragedy. And although we were the only Protestants, we were accepted as one of the family.

"My grandparents in Woodbury were friendly enough but you really had to behave when you visited them. That was easy for me. I knew what people wanted me to do and I accommodated them.

"We were very poor when I was a child. We didn't have indoor plumbing until I was 10 years old. My parents worked in factories, they said, so that my sister and I could have a better life. I didn't have much interaction with other kids and felt like an outsider in almost any social environment.

"My father had a bad temper and strong opinions about the ways things should be. I had a great fear of doing the wrong thing, whatever that was. If I was 'bad' he would lose his temper and yell at me and give me a licking, usually with a yardstick." Mike pauses, "I hated that yardstick!

"I was always made conscious of how I was behaving because 'people are watching you,' and 'what will people think?' I remember watching my father when he lost his temper and thinking how foolish he looked.

"My mother was a lady with dignity and class, but passive. She didn't talk about how she was feeling, and from her I soon learned to stuff my anger deep inside."

Mike still wants to please people and avoids confrontation. He confesses to having difficulty if he thinks people don't like him.

"Along the way, I developed a sense of humor. I see a lot in life that is genuinely funny—not dark, gallows humor, or slapstick, but the subtle things in life. Humor is one thing I don't have to stuff inside. But I still have a conscious or unconscious awareness of molding my actions to conform to others' expectations. In my story, that is a very important—in fact, crucial—element."

Except for about two dates in high school, Mike did not date. Not that he didn't want to, but he wasn't sure any girl would want to go out with him. If one did, he was afraid he would say "something stupid," and it would get around and the kids would make fun of him.

"I longed to have a girlfriend," Mike remembers from this time in his life. "It wasn't until I was a sophomore in college that some of my friends set me up on a blind date—with Rachel. It seemed safe enough since we were going out with friends.

"Rachel was quiet and friendly and we started dating regularly. I found out she had had a lot of boyfriends in the past and I could hardly believe that she wanted to go steady with me. I was smitten! In fact, I was seriously beginning to think about marriage when, one evening after we had dated for nine months, she told me that she was seeing one of her old boyfriends and it was over with us." Mike smiles ruefully, "I was devastated, and any confidence I had begun to feel about women vanished! For the next two years I didn't date anyone. Then I got a letter from Rachel asking me to the spring dance.

"I must admit I thought long and hard about that one. I had this feeling I might fall for her again and, sure enough, I did. We saw each other often that summer and after I left for basic training, we wrote every day. That was hard, but by Thanksgiving I had proposed to her and we set the wedding date for Christmas. I was elated!

During the next two years they moved to Corpus Christi, then to Minneapolis and finally to England. "I flew into London on Christmas eve," Rachel recalls. "We had been separated for four months and I couldn't wait to see him! We went looking for a flat to make our own home. We didn't have much money then, but we had each other. It sounds a little hokey now, but it was true. We played monopoly and pinochle on cold, wet, winter nights and even managed to do some traveling in Europe."

At the end of two years there, they returned to Twin Falls, Mike's hometown, and lived with his parents until they found an apartment of their own. They both began working and eventually started a family.

They had a beautiful, healthy baby boy, full of energy and

excitement. He was bright and learned quickly and easily. Another son was born about two years later—and surprise—nineteen months later they became parents to a daughter. "I had three children in diapers for a while, and at times it overwhelmed me. I was a fanatic about keeping the house immaculate and had a schedule for doing everything. I was a real superwoman!" Rachel laughs. "I did everything for everybody because it was easier that way; then it was done the way I wanted it done."

Many times at the end of the day Mike wanted to be affectionate and loving, but Rachel was too tired and too irritated to respond. "Regretfully," Rachel says, "I wasn't able to relax with Mike, or even communicate with him much. And I took little time to play with the children."

For Mike this recalled some of their earlier experiences. He had been "surprised and disappointed" during their honeymoon when she did not want to have sex, saying she was "too tired." "At the time I chalked it up to the exhausting events of the wedding, but as the years went by she became less and less interested in being intimate in any way. At times when she worked in the kitchen I wanted to be close to her. I would give her a hug and kiss her; she would stamp her foot and say, 'You know I can't stand that!' If I wanted sex more than once a week, I was made to feel as though I was too demanding, so I came to accept it. I learned to push the desire for intimacy and closeness, not necessarily sex, deep inside me."

However, they both remember those first years of their marriage as good ones. They didn't fight over money or argue like they saw other couples do. "I believe I was becoming so good at stuffing down my disappointments and anger that no one could really tell how I was feeling. I couldn't even admit it to myself," Mike says thoughtfully.

Their oldest son did well in school, but it soon became apparent that the two younger children had difficulty in their studies. "From the time they entered school, the struggles never stopped. Jeff was transferred out of the regular school because of his learning disability. Betsy continued to have difficulty that no one could understand or explain. They were shipped around the county by bus to wherever the powers-that-be thought they should go," Rachel remembers.

"After multitudes of tests and never-ending visits to many doctors, our daughter was diagnosed as having Tourette's Syndrome, a neurological disease characterized by facial grimaces, tics and involuntary arm and shoulder movements. She was often placed where she really didn't belong, with children who had behavior problems. We despaired of getting her into the right class for help, in spite of the fact that we had numerous counseling sessions, always trying to understand if we were doing something wrong and what could be done.

"Often Mike and I disagreed on how things should be handled. Other times we rallied together, intent on carrying out the crusade to meet the special educational needs our children had. Every year we went to meetings, ever campaigning for something better for them."

Mike remembers the unending doctors, the dashed hopes and the many disagreements he and Rachel had over the right course to take. Always beneath it all, was their profound sadness for the lost dreams for their children, their development and happiness.

Jeff and Betsy struggled through high school, often ridiculed by other children on the bus and in their classrooms. "We agonized for them and for ourselves over the injustices and unfairness of what we were experiencing," Rachel says, still with a residue of hurt and anger.

Their oldest son completed high school, went on to college and graduated there with honors. He got a good job with a wide range of benefits. Then as he grew older, he began telling Rachel and Mike how much he resented all the time and effort they put into the two younger children when he was still at home. "We were so caught up in our quest for Jeff's and Betsy's rights that we missed seeing life from Doug's perspective. He always did so well, it was easy to overlook his need for us. He began rebelling in ways that were difficult for us to deal with," Rachel observes with some sorrow.

Doug married a young woman who was bright, friendly and articulate. Unfortunately, she also had frequent migraine headaches and became addicted to pain medications. Although they all tried to help in the best way they knew, they were unable to make enough of a difference. She and Doug had a son, Rachel and Mike's only grandchild. Sadly, however, when he was only four years old, his mother died of an overdose of medications.

Since then Doug has gone from one relationship to another and is now married for the third time. But Rachel and Mike's grief does not end there.

About three years ago, Doug was admitted to a psychiatric unit for the fourth time in one 12-month period. Mike explains a devastating event that happened during that time. "I thought we had kept a pretty healthy relationship with him, in spite of the hurt he experienced when we were so involved with the two younger children. But I wasn't prepared for what was to come.

"Rachel and I were called in for a meeting, and Doug, reading from notes he had written, stated that he had been physically and mentally abused by us, that my uncle had sexually abused him, that we were a sick family and that he wanted no more contact with us."

Mike still has difficulty talking about this now, the pain is so great. "I know that I was too strict a father in some matters, and likely not strict enough in others. I thought we had been quite generous; we did pay all his schooling. It seemed to me the older he got, the better the relationship with us became. So we were almost destroyed. He completely estranged himself from us.

"My impulse was to be strong and stay rational. Rachel thought we should sue for the custody of Doug's son. I was deeply hurt by Doug's rejection and angry at the way Rachel and the rest of our family were being so unreasonable. No one seemed to care how I felt. I guess we were each dealing with the chaos and surprise in our own way. I just stuffed my feelings inside," Mike acknowledges.

Doug now allows them to see their grandson for a few hours every three weeks and for one week in the summer. Although they enjoy these brief periods of time with him, the whole experience has been especially difficult since they had delighted in grandparenting and in his earlier regular visits.

"We have written frequent letters," Rachel explains, "begging

Doug's doctors to help bring our family together so we can work at whatever the issues are, but to no avail.

"Our second son, Jeff, graduated from high school, then faced a terrible time fitting into a job. No one wanted him because he could not work fast enough. He tried job after job, often coming home hurt and angry because someone had spoken harshly to him, impatient that he couldn't keep up with the work, not understanding the pressure he experienced.

"Finally, Goodwill Industries, through their program for adults with learning disabilities, assisted him in finding a position he now holds with pride and satisfaction—working in a department store. Two years ago he met and married a fine young woman who has similar interests and abilities. They are making each other happy and are a real bright spot in our lives," Rachel says proudly.

"Our daughter also graduated from high school and works in the kitchen of a large restaurant. She has only a few friends because she is so self-conscious about the symptoms which her illness causes. She did learn to drive," Rachel offers with pleasure, "and at age 25 had the self-confidence to move into her own apartment. She goes to school three nights a week, training to be a hair stylist, but she continues to struggle socially. Still, we're pleased with the progress she's making."

Rachel continues with her story. "Mike and I struggled for years with our children's needs. Now we are alone together. Often we were at odds with each other regarding the children. Sometimes I felt torn between the children and Mike, but I couldn't talk to him about it. I wish we had paid more attention to each other. Instead of communicating on a deeper level, we were two 'nice' people who never fought, trying to raise our children in the best way we could."

Rachel acknowledges she was seldom able to enjoy the present, that she was always needing to anticipate the future. "Mike hated my negative outlook on everything. I tried to change but I couldn't. And so I felt guilty."

The stress eventually caught up with Mike physically. He was hospitalized with acute hemorrhagic gastritis, a quite painful condition. "The doctor asked me if I drank coffee or alcohol since my stomach looked like an old man's. Then he asked me if I was under stress. Stress? What stress? I had stuffed everything so deep inside that I was not aware of it."

Mike finally visited a counselor to help in sorting out all that was going on in his life. He didn't have the courage to tell Rachel about his appointment until the night before the first session. "I thought that if she knew earlier, she would want answers and I didn't have any."

The work Rachel and Mike eventually did together in counseling proved to be a period of intense discovery. "The emotions I had bottled up all began to come out," says Mike. "I never cried like I did then; I felt I was finally starting to be free. Although I could see the absolute agony and anguish on Rachel's face, I couldn't seem to bring back that loving feeling I had lost longer ago than I care to remember. I was tempted to start stuffing my feelings again because if I said everything was all right, her pain would go away, but I couldn't do that anymore."

✦

Mike kept a journal during their week of Recovery of Hope:

"**June 13**—Observing and understanding our family histories helps me to have insight into why Rachel and I react to situations the way we do. While I believe you can't blame your parents for how you have been affected, nevertheless it is important to understand and recognize the effects. The thing I have to think about is what have I done with my own children? I said today that I can't remember my parents hugging me or telling me they loved me, although I know they did. But I think I made the same mistake with our own children.

"**June 14**—In psychodrama today, it was difficult for me to look at someone playing my role. They did it accurately and it was a jolt. They told me they didn't want to hear all my words anymore, and that hurt. But I guess the truth hurts. I don't want to hurt people because I don't want to be seen as the bad guy. Somehow I need to focus on making myself a genuine and better person.

"**June 15**—I told a story today that I've told many times but through it came a moment of truth. Suddenly I saw the connections between that and how I've suppressed so many things. I couldn't go on, and all the weariness and grief and sadness of a life of carrying around these burdens overwhelmed me, and I broke down and cried.

"**June 16**—We have the morning to ourselves. I see the agony and anguish Rachel is going through. I remember a gift that Doug had given us one Christmas. It was a clock on an embroidered background that said, "Plant me a garden to heal the soul." He knew that I was an avid gardener. How now do I heal my soul? How can I heal my soul when I cause anguish to others?

"**June 17**—Rachel and I took a walk in the park today. We sat down at a picnic table in the pine grove. I told Rachel that I can't stand the anguish I'm causing any longer. I compared myself to being in a china shop. I go around and smash all the china and then as I'm walking out I say, "Now I feel better." I finished saying all this and then I began to cry. We started to walk and I began crying again. I could not stop. I remember saying, 'I don't want to carry this anymore,' and I can't. I honestly believe I can be a nice person but I'm tired of feeling like I *have* to.

"**June 18**—This afternoon the session was very intense. A lot of anger came out from both Rachel and me. I didn't realize I had so much stored up inside against her.

"**June 19**—I think I will take a month away from home by myself in the near future. I need some time for reflection. I feel kind of numb this evening, drained.

"**June 20**—It's been almost a week of dealing with some pretty crucial issues. Last evening we met with Pat and Sam and told them some of our story. That felt good. There is a time when persons have to focus on themselves and their own struggles, but I believe I must also start to reach out beyond myself.

"**July 29**—[After Mike was away for almost a month, helping with a work project as well as spending time alone.] It's a Saturday morning and I have just returned from a walk on the beach. It was so soothing and relaxing, watching the sunrise, listening to tapes. I thought how lucky I am to be able to hear and see such beauty. I thought of the healing that has taken place over the last few weeks and I cried. I am mentally and emotionally ready to return home to Rachel. I don't know what that will all mean, but I think I'm ready to live with a different outlook and attitude.

"I dreamed more this past month than I have in the last few years. I don't know what the significance is. I would wake up and think, 'I have to react differently in this situation.' It was like critiquing a video of yourself.

"I have decided that God made me who I am and I don't have to be perfect. I don't have to stuff all my emotions inside. I don't have to take everything on my shoulders. I can stop sometimes and smell the flowers and observe the butterflies. People care; they matter. There's no good reason to feel insecure. I don't have to get uptight when things don't go right. I can't be all things to all people. I can be me and that's not so bad!"

◆

Meanwhile Rachel worked at her own agenda in different ways at home. Although she was lonely at times, she understood the benefit of being separate for a while. "I think Mike has a hard time believing that I will change, too. I know I already have, but I have far to go. I used to depend on Mike for so many things. Now I'm learning to stand on my own two feet. We have had lots of fights, arguments and intense discussions, trying to understand each other and arrive at decisions and answers for us. I think we are going to make it!"

The issues and events Rachel and Mike have lived with have caused many couples to give up on each other. Not only has each had to overcome a debilitating childhood and adolescence with their far–reaching effects, the two of them live with ongoing hurt in their own immediate family. What dynamics occur in a family when there are children with special needs?

Whether the difficult problems with children are emotional, physical or intellectual, parents may form coalitions that can become dysfunctional. For example, one parent may become the learning disabled child's advocate, explaining and excusing the child to the other parent. (Many times this forms between the mother and child, although not necessarily.) This coalition becomes dysfunctional when it weakens the bond between husband and wife. This is especially true when there is already distance and hurt between them.

While there can be great benefit for the child when one of the parents works especially well in assisting, teaching and disciplining that child, the other parent can understandably feel inadequate or left out. Parents who are aware of this dynamic can assist each other in their different roles with the child. If the bonding and support between parents is clear and apparent, the child will also be more comfortable.

All of us find ourselves caught on occasion between two highly important commitments, both of which claim us at the same time. When the conflict of commitment is between one's spouse and the care of one's children, especially children who, as in Rachel and Mike's case, require an inestimable investment of physical and emotional energy, the dilemma becomes particularly unique and difficult.

One feels caught between what one *should* do and what one *can* do. Many times such situations ask for more than anyone can deliver. The question changes, then, to one of caring: can we, do we, care enough to find our way through the conflicts which two commitments present? Mike and Rachel are an example of two who do.

15

It Was a Miracle

Certain times and experiences in our lives make us wish for a miracle to spirit us away from the misery and pain that threaten us. We long for a miracle to take the hurt away, to restore things to the way they used to be, to simply but completely change the present. On rare occasions events occur which are difficult to explain in terms other than the transcendent. Miracles sometimes do happen, according to Martin's and Sue's story.

"Our life as a couple began more than 30 years ago during our last two years of high school," Martin begins. "Our relationship developed without any unusual problems. We spent the first five years in Colorado, 600 miles from home. We filled our time with each other, starting a family, being busy with church, college and work. Sue and I believed we had a one-of-a-kind relationship. While we had our disagreements, we were usually calm and understanding and able to anticipate each others' needs almost instinctively.

"After college, we returned to Arizona and settled into a typical young family routine. Over a period of 10 years our family grew to include three sons, and our schedules grew more complex and demanding. We stepped up our involvement in many activities, all of them good, but all of them ultimately allowing less and less time for Sue and me as a couple.

"We moved along though, dreaming about calmer times to come. Our marriage seemed to float along, experiencing no major low points, nor major high points either, except the births of our children.

"In Sue's effort to manage our busy schedule, I started to feel controlled and then resentful of her and her ever-present list of 'things to do.' But I kept silent, thinking that she would soon see what was happening and make some changes.

"I moved from slight irritation to a rut of complacency that soon began to take its toll on our relationship. My job was also settling into the dull and routine. Like our marriage, it seemed to be going nowhere. I was fast approaching a dead end. My discouragements built as it became clear that I would have no further advancement in my present job.

"I decided to take some additional college business courses, thinking that that might enhance my future. I was not disappointed. I was soon approached by a company noted for its rapid growth rate, with an irresistible offer. A career change at 36! No mid-life crisis for me."

Martin moved up into new and more energizing, as well as demanding, areas of the company. Work required more and more of his time including occasional late nights. But his excitement about carrying such significant responsibility overshadowed the trade-off he subtly sensed he was making—less time with Sue and with their boys. "We unwittingly traded away our closeness so we could accommodate all the other demands we had allowed to pressure us," Martin summarizes with obvious regret.

"I noticed Martin's growing lack of interest in me and our sons, but I was unable to pinpoint the problem," Sue recalls. "I did not foresee the severity of our coming problems; I assumed our marriage was forever. Although I still felt comfortable with our relationship, I was beginning to feel I couldn't communicate with Martin. If I initiated a conversation or suggested an activity it would noticeably irritate him. I rationalized that it was normal during these busy years of balancing teenagers and schedules.

"While I had always done part-time substitute teaching, I started teaching full-time as the boys hit high school. That was an adjustment. I was at school by 7:15 a.m. Home again by 3:45 p.m., for another eight hours of work: cooking, cleaning, washing and ironing, transporting sons to oboe, piano and guitar lessons, ball practice and gymnastics, helping with homework, packing lunches, and the list went on. I literally dropped into bed at 11:30 p.m. Family communication was reduced to a 'list of things to do' left on the dining room table.

"I didn't deny it was a heavy schedule, but it seemed normal for a growing family. I unconsciously gave little attention to our marriage, assuming it would wait while we raised our children. I believed our main responsibilities were guiding our children through this time of their development."

Martin recalls feeling let down after a year or two of excitement in his new job. Pressures at work and demands at home consumed his energy. He remembers loneliness and the hope for some return of the spark in their marriage. "I saw the chrome of our once shining marriage slowly rusting away. We were ignoring the polishing that our emotional, spiritual and physical well-being required.

"I remembered how carefree things used to be," Martin says. "Our spontaneity and fun had been replaced by so much tense responsibility. We had no time for silliness. It began to feel like such an effort to have to tell Sue what I needed, and then to have to repeat it all again the next time. I thought we had lived together long enough that Sue should sense my needs automatically."

Martin began to wonder if the magic of their early relationship was just an illusion. "Maybe it was never true to begin with. Maybe this whole thing was a total mistake. If Sue was going to persist in overlooking my needs, she obviously didn't care enough to *want* to make me happy. I decided to stay on my side on the fence and shout back in silence. I suppose I was getting even," Martin concludes.

Martin's distance did not go unnoticed by Sue. She too, was feeling lonely and unappreciated. "In fact, I was getting the impression from Martin that I never did anything right. Silence was becoming his way of dealing with a problem. If he did say anything, it was sharp and accusingly spoken. I could not tolerate silence very well and many times I translated it into feeling rejected."

"My major concern quickly became that of myself, *my* happiness, deciding what I wanted from life and what to do about it," Martin remembers. "My family was tying me down and Sue didn't want to be creative enough to keep me interested. Soon I saw any reminders about my responsibilities at home or relationships with the family as encroachments on my needs as an individual.

"I skirted my commitments at home by blaming the people I saw standing in the way of my happiness. I began to feel as though I needed to be someone other than who I was in order to live with this family. Any good memories I had about our marriage faded and then disappeared, as though they had never existed.

"One day someone came into my life with much the same kinds of problems and needs as mine. The timing couldn't have been much better. We were both vulnerable, and we quickly learned that we could console each other about these disappointments in our lives. We understood each other almost immediately. It was a comfortable, no-strings-attached friendship which took away some of the loneliness we were feeling. A friendship only. Nothing more.

"Our relationship grew. Soon we had longer and deeper eye contact. Then a birthday kiss. A New Year's kiss. Since we worked closely together, we discovered we had the same professional experiences. We shared our ideas and concerns; we worked toward the same business goals, communicating freely about our work projects.

"We were around each other during the most productive parts of our days, alert and poised. We accepted each other at face value, constantly amazed at how quickly we learned to do those things that pleased the other. We shared unconditionally, making walls or fences unnecessary.

"Subtly at first, but with each day our feelings for each other grew stronger and stronger until they replaced anything either of us believed we had at home. We felt completely compatible. We had the same tastes and interests. We didn't have to push or pull to get a response from the other; many times we seemed to read each other's thoughts. We didn't need to guard our words or curb our actions. We were simply spontaneous and tender to each other. Our time together extended into lunches, noontime walks around town and finally after-work hours. We each continued to discover the other, enjoying what we found. In seven months we had fallen in love."

There wasn't much left at home for Martin compared to what was coming so effortlessly for him with this special woman. He remembers feeling as though his world started to spin again. He had found a beautiful relationship. "Deep, down inside though, I knew it was wrong. It was the beginning of terrible emotional struggles for me. But I managed to justify my feelings for her," Martin says.

His late nights away from home soon became commonplace. "Sue sat by the window waiting for me to arrive, no matter whether it was 10:00 p.m. or 1:00 a.m., and she would readily accept my explanation for being late. She succeeded in silently sending me on a guilt trip. It made me angry. Was she so incredibly naive? Couldn't she see what she was allowing me to do? How could I care if she didn't?" Big questions and rationalization helped Martin take the next steps.

Quickly he placed more distance between himself and his family in order to move on to what he was determined to have.

"My new love and I decided that if our spouses could see how happy we were with each other, and if they really loved us, they would release us from our marriage commitments and let us go.

"We were so much in love, so starved for affection that we quickly anticipated our future together. We had become so totally committed to each other that we were ready to start over completely. We knew we would probably be asked to leave the company, but if we were prepared to walk away from our families, that adjustment would be minor by comparison.

"We began to act more openly with our emotions. Our relationship was becoming obvious to the people in our office, but by that time we didn't really care what others thought. We were bonding and building strength in a way we felt had never existed with our spouses. We bolstered our commitment by finally telling each other, *and truly believing it,* that we simply never loved the people we married. Our marriages were mistakes from the beginning!"

Sue remembers those times quite clearly. "On Monday night, July 16, I tried to interest Martin in lovemaking. Not only did he flatly reject my advances, he seemed almost angry at me for wanting to be intimate. His response was unbearable; I needed him so much. I asked him what I had done wrong—again. Finally after a long and lonely silence he said, 'I can't postpone the inevitable any longer. I can't stay here.'"

Sue recalls being shaken totally off balance. In a few days they were to leave for a two-week family vacation to California. Talking further simply brought deeper hurt. "Through my tears and panic during the next three hours I realized that he was dead serious! He wanted to leave that night but stayed. We finally fell asleep but only for an hour. The radio awakened me, playing, ironically, 'Please Release Me, Let Me Go.' Martin was awake and I asked him, 'That's what you want, isn't it?' 'Yes,' he answered."

Sue had never thought that separation and divorce would be an issue for her and Martin. That only happened to others. She had always believed there were solutions to any problems they might face.

"But now I felt such despair that I knew we needed help. That same Tuesday morning I called a counselor. We were in his office by 9:00 a.m. Martin didn't talk about his other relationship during that session. In fact, I didn't find out about it until Wednesday night. Immediately I felt guilty for spending too much of my time on things other than our marriage.

"I still believed we could work things out, until he told me how much he really loved 'her' and not me. He said he could not continue wearing a mask to protect my feelings from being hurt. I held up until thoughts of the future flooded my mind. What would this mean to our children? We hadn't even allowed them to watch soap operas because of the lifestyles they portrayed. How could we ever celebrate birthdays, graduations, weddings? We had always been a family who looked for reasons to celebrate. Now life seemed to end for me."

Martin tried to convince Sue that their life together had been a terrible mistake, a sham that could no longer be fabricated. "What hurt me so badly," Sue continues, "was when Martin told me that he had always pretended happiness and that little in our lives together really meant anything to him. I couldn't believe that all our happy times had meant nothing—our college years, our vacations, the births of our children, cards and flowers. He had even remembered our anniversary *every month*. Now 'nothing?' He said he was sorry but he couldn't continue this charade any longer."

What followed for Sue were sleepless nights and depressing days. She had no appetite and lost 10 pounds in five days. "Although I continued to teach and tried to relate to the children, I carried a heavy feeling on my chest and a tightness in my throat. I was constantly on edge, and frightened of the future which threatened to vaporize at any moment."

Meanwhile Martin gave more and more details about his other relationship in order to convince Sue of his intentions. "I saw Sue losing her grip on reality and feared she was headed for a breakdown. It was obvious that she needed help yet that night. The least I could do was call for an appointment with a counselor immediately. After she calmed down we managed to weather another night—in separate rooms.

"When we were in the counseling session Sue said she could accept this turn of events better if I would be willing to work at saving the marriage. She couldn't understand why I didn't even want to work things out. So I decided to at least go through the motions of salvaging things in order to satisfy Sue's need. I certainly had no plans to change my mind.

"I had, by this time, told our oldest son of my plans, indicating to him as lovingly as I could that his mother's and my relationship was beyond repair. Sue told the other children what was happening to us. Our middle child just sat around staring blankly into space. Our youngest was totally confused and scared of being abandoned, crying himself to sleep. I was given the job of helping him settle down at night. Sue thought this would turn me around out of compassion, if I saw what I was doing to this little one. But I was so set in my direction that it did not produce the reaction for which Sue had hoped. I had already prepared myself for those kinds of mental conflicts."

On Thursday morning Sue received a call from the counselor asking whether the two of them would consider going to a program designed for troubled marriages. Still looking for anything that might save their marriage, Sue convinced Martin that he should go with her. He went, he says, "with the intention of ending the marriage. At least she would be with people who could help her cope with the eventual outcome."

Martin's boss was understanding and more than willing to allow him time off for the Recovery of Hope week, to "get this thing straightened out." When Martin told his lover about the trip, she was frightened about the prospect of being left alone and of losing him through what she felt would be the "brainwashing" efforts of a center dedicated to saving marriages. He needed to go through it so Sue would be taken care of, he explained, and "so our love can weather this storm and prove our rightness for each other."

He left her with tears, but before they parted, she gave him a symbol representing their future together, a single, delicate, yellow daisy.

Sue wanted to inform their family and several of their close friends about their plans. "First they asked if we were all packed for California. When I told them we were on our way to a marriage clinic instead, they wondered what on earth for! Our parents were stunned but managed to pray for us, trusting that things would work out. None of our immediate friends guessed what was happening to us. Knowing few details, they all promised us their thoughts and prayers.

"Saturday morning at the introductory session we listened to stories of three troubled marriages which were reconciled. I was having problems relating our lives to those giving their stories. It was not what I had in mind as a method for turning our marriage around!" Sue recalls with some derisiveness.

"I knew Martin was skeptical anyway and probably not ready to hear anything about reconciliation, especially in the manner it was being presented. I was let down because I was sure he was being turned off completely by what he was hearing. I felt terribly alone. Here I was among strangers, a thousand miles from home and family. Why did all this have to happen to us?" Sue remembers the painful questions that raced through her mind.

Even so, Sue still hoped something would make a difference

for them. She had not given up. But when they were asked to write reflections about their marriage and Martin stated his goal to end the marriage *now*, her hope started to dwindle. She felt utter disbelief at hearing his intentions put so coldly. Martin remained unmoved and determined.

That afternoon Sue learned additional details about Martin's other relationship. He was trying to make Sue accept the situation without telling more than he felt was necessary. "As the day wore on Martin widened the chasm between us by revealing the remainder of his dark secrets from the previous seven months. He apparently needed to give me more and more facts in order to convince me that our marriage was really over. My hope lasted through Saturday evening, even with all this added information and hurt," Sue recalls.

"When I awoke Sunday," Sue continues, "I felt a deep rejection, a sharp sense of loss. I know now that I had given up. It was over. I realized that I could not live with Martin knowing that his heart was not with me. We had to do something but I didn't know what.

"I got up and went to the kitchen of our host home where I found a pot of coffee, two mugs and a bowl of fruit, along with two handwritten notes and a church bulletin. One note was an invitation to attend our host couple's church. The other was an invitation to have Sunday dinner with them.

"Although I didn't feel like going to church, I knew we couldn't stay in the house. When I asked Martin to get out of bed, he replied strongly, 'You can't tell me what to do!' For the first time I let my anger show. I literally pulled him out of bed."

"I knew Sue was angry," Martin remembers that interchange, "because after I stated that she couldn't tell me what to do, she threw a pillow at me! It may as well have been the refrigerator. She never yelled at anyone, let alone threw things. Her gesture displayed uncommon anger. I was up, after her hard physical and verbal pull. We would be going to church."

When Martin saw the notes on the table, he immediately suspected a set-up. He checked the sermon title, then quickly looked for a Bible so he could prepare a "defense strategy" ahead of time. The sermon was entitled "Proposal at the Threshing

Floor," based on the book of Ruth in the Old Testament. He read the entire chapter but couldn't see any connection to a brain-washing maneuver, so he quickly read other chapters just in case he was missing something. He laughs now, recalling the moment. "I still wasn't sure how this could be a threat to me, but I felt better having done a little studying before hand."

When they arrived at the church, an usher seated them halfway up the center aisle, not a location they would have chosen under the circumstances. "But I didn't feel like protesting in public, so we stayed there," Martin says. "Everything seemed like a set-up to me, even the hymns they chose, and I began to feel very uncomfortable."

As the service progressed, Martin became more and more uneasy. "I was sure I would lose my composure at any minute," he says. "Then I remembered that I had just what I needed right there with me. I took the daisy from my billfold and held it tightly in my hand. It represented everything that I would have to give up, should I succumb to what I perceived as pressure. I was strengthened by the thought and felt better, but only for a moment.

"The service seemed to end abruptly. The minister moved to the back of the church where he gave the benediction. As people began to move out into the aisle, a lady seated next to us wanted to visit. I received her warm greetings with mixed feelings. I had a compelling need to get away!

"I grabbed Sue's hand and I stepped out into the center aisle, but instead of leaving I was suddenly being drawn toward the front of the church!" Martin remembers with disbelief. "Sue, not knowing what was happening, held on as we moved in the opposite direction of everyone else.

"As we approached the Communion table at the front of the church, my eyes were drawn to the open Bible and flower arrangement placed upon a pure white cloth covering the table. I stopped. The voice I heard in my head was unmistakable! *This is too much for you to carry. Put it here and I'll take care of it.*'

"I found myself reaching out, placing my hand over the table and releasing the daisy onto the white cloth. I recall touching it one last time before I turned away.

Recovery of Hope

"I pulled Sue across the church and we entered a door marked 'Prayer Room.' The room was empty but when we walked in we found ourselves in the middle of an awakening in our lives. I saw Sue in a new way. Through an outpouring of emotion and tears, my tons of guilt and despair and darkness washed away. God's forgiveness and Sue's forgiveness filled the room. Our sudden ability to forgive and to be forgiven brought us back to each other. We sensed God's presence deeply as we held each other there. There was a blackboard and on it I wrote the words, 'I want you.'

"I don't know how long we were there holding each other, but when we opened the door everyone else was gone. We walked out of that church and into the brightest sunshine I can ever remember. We and our marriage had been reborn," Martin says, recalling the sacredness of that occasion.

During the week following that Sunday, Sue and Martin worked hard with their counselors at putting their relationship into perspective. "We learned what drove us apart and what we needed to deal with in the difficult times we were certain would come along. It was the beginning of many new and exciting things about each other. We began learning to *give* more than we expected to receive."

"In the beginning we had fallen in love. Seventeen years later I experienced falling out of love. I realize," Martin continues, "that selfish reasoning and lack of deep communication caused me to make the choice I did. Now we have made new choices. We look for opportunities to learn more about each other. When we decided to work at really being married and not just 'wed,' we saved all the history we had built together and rediscovered the excitement that had disappeared from our marriage. More importantly, we see a promising future unfolding before us. We are enjoying what *real* love is all about," Martin says with enthusiasm.

"I know that Martin and I each experienced a miracle," Sue adds. "I don't know how else to explain it. It was a miracle that we could give and receive forgiveness so quickly and completely. I know it doesn't happen that way in a lot of circumstances.

"We are indeed two changed people. We are a changed family. We now realize what is required in order to continue growing in our marriage. We have replaced mind reading with honest communication. We have learned how to express our feelings to each other without guilt and without conveying resistance or rejection. And because we can now say *no* honestly and freely, we find it so much easier to want to say *yes* and still maintain our individual integrity, even when it means compromise.

"We know," Sue concludes, "that the fulfillment of our lives together will not come about by chance. Marriage is a living thing. It requires commitment, attention, loving care and God."

"Love is a decision," Martin adds emphatically. "For me it has become a flame which burns brighter than ever before. Our children have seen it and have learned from it, too."

There is obviously in Martin and Sue's relationship a profound appreciation and respect for each other and the miracle they experienced.

16

Whose Fault Was It?

Sandy speaks first. "I remember that I was reading aloud to the family after dinner one day when I was still in elementary school. I must have made some mistakes because my father ridiculed me in front of everyone. That happened with many of the activities I was involved in. I became almost frightened to participate in things that required verbal or athletic skills," she says.

"I guess I still feel that way as an adult. Recently I told Dad that he should be proud of me now that I have finally learned to swim. Here I am, still looking for his approval, but he didn't even care enough to respond. Nothing. I was crushed! I heard the old messages of being–a–failure–without–much–worth playing in my head again."

Sandy remembers her mother tiptoeing around the house, trying to keep peace with everyone. "Anger was not an acceptable emotion in our house, except with Dad. I remember him becoming angry only three times but then he lay down on the floor and kicked his hands and feet like a child having a tantrum. The tension was so thick I could touch it.

"We didn't discuss any feelings at home, so we spent a lot of time guessing what everyone else was thinking and feeling. I remember when my friend's father died. I had known him only a short time but he had been a special person to me. I tried to tell my mother how I felt, but she couldn't understand. I ended up going to a neighbor for comfort."

"I guess it wasn't that different for me," Matt adds, with pensive longing. "I never heard if I did something right. I learned soon enough to protect myself from any emotional hurt, so I just didn't allow myself to feel much of anything. That way it didn't hurt."

In Sandy's family love was something you earned. You received it if you acted in the correct way. "I had to kiss my dad good-night even when I was 15 years old and there was a house full of guests, or I didn't receive his love. As I came to understand that I could never measure up to what my parents wanted, I felt more and more worthless."

Another message played loudly in Sandy's family: no matter what Grandpop did or how he treated people, he was right and must be obeyed. This carried over into another painful experience for Sandy.

"I spent a month-long vacation with my aunt one summer when I was just a young girl. While I was there my grandfather also came to visit them. He molested me on a number of occasions during that time," Sandy recalls with deep anger. "Each night I would lose my voice around 7:00 and wouldn't be able to speak till morning. I also got hives each evening for the rest of the summer. Sex was never discussed in our family, so how could I have begun to tell anyone what had happened? Grandfather seemed to be God, and so I pushed it all from my consciousness.

"As I grew older, I only knew that I didn't want to spend time with my mother's parents. I remember once when Grandfather drove me home from school. I can tell you about every turn on that long, long ride home," the fear in Sandy's voice even now reveals her panic of being alone with her grandfather.

No one seemed to notice her fear and discomfort. In time she sought safety and developed strong emotional ties with her pastor and his wife. They became her best friends, ones with whom she could talk. They made her feel safe and protected, while her parents often made her feel guilty about not wanting to be with her own family, especially her grandparents.

"When Grandpop died, no one could have understood how I felt. How dared I say that I was glad he was dead. I didn't know how to admit that to myself or to understand the sense of relief I felt. I had a lot of things stuffed 'way back in my mind."

Matt found Sandy accepting of him when they began dating. "She took me just the way I was—no conditions. We were comfortable with each other; we could talk about anything, or at least it seemed that way. All the things I wanted in a marriage, unlike my own parents', I felt I had found in Sandy.

"My father was an alcoholic and I was determined to not have a home like the one from which I came. Sandy and I were developing such a comfortable relationship that I thought this was it."

Matt knows now that wanting a marriage different from one's parents', and succeeding at creating such a relationship, requires more than desire and even intention. Spouses, shaped by their families of origin, inevitably bring their childhood experiences into their marriages. Many of us are unable alone to recognize potential problems. Matt and Sandy's marriage has been a long journey in understanding what each brought to their relationship.

Sandy can now talk about her strong sense of guilt and shame, as well as her mistrust of men. "I was continually made to do things out of guilt. I would go out with the son of my mother's friend because he was short and didn't have a date. I realize now that it was also a way for me to play safe. I was afraid to come to love someone because look what happened with Grandpop. I trusted him and see how he betrayed me."

Matt had a different kind of impulse. "Even though I wanted to do things with Sandy, because I never knew what that was like in my family, I also had an unspoken rule in my head—what I wanted to do was my decision, regardless of the circumstances. A wife simply had to adjust to that. That was part of being married," Matt explains with regret.

"I love sports, especially hunting. Sandy was taught that such things were a waste of time. Our son was born about three weeks before hunting season one fall, so her mother came to stay with her while I went hunting for four days. I didn't understand how that made Sandy feel, and we did not have the skills to talk about it."

"It was hard enough that he didn't want to stay home with me. But then my mother let me know that, although she enjoyed being with me and the baby, Matt's place was at home working. Work, work, work. My family were workaholics! But I also thought I couldn't be very important to Matt if he wasn't willing to give up hunting just this one time."

Sandy kept trying to talk things out, but always stopped short of saying how really angry she was because she believed that would have been wrong. Usually she would say she was hurt, then skirt around the topic in lots of ways without expressing her feelings accurately. The harder she tried to tell Matt about how she was feeling, the more withdrawn he became, falling into the familiar, although lonely, pattern of protecting himself. Sandy interpreted his response as her own failure, never able to measure up, always being worthless.

"I remember a time when I had completely redecorated our home and everyone but Matt said it was lovely. I was undone. I wanted to know that what I did was not only lovely, but mattered to him. The secret I never told him was that it was a gift from me to him, something I had wanted to do especially for him."

Sandy poured herself into school and community activities where she received some affirmation. Meanwhile, things at home did not improve. They had differences everywhere—in child-rearing practices, discipline, expectations of each other, and on the list went. Matt became more and more distant.

One event accentuated the growing alienation between them. Their daughter Cheryl had become quite attractive and was active in school and in church. Increasingly she became attached to the youth leader at church who was much older than she. Sandy was disturbed by the young man because she thought his behavior was inappropriate with the youth in general.

"Cheryl seemed to be infatuated with him," Sandy recalls. "Matt thought I was overly concerned but agreed to talk with him. I continued to have a feeling that something was quite wrong. Eventually we found out the very painful fact that Joel, the youth leader, had molested her. I was outraged! It brought back with a vengeance all my awful childhood experiences. What's more, when I felt I needed Matt the most, he was unable to respond to me.

"I blamed Matt for not picking up on my earlier anxiety about Cheryl. Not only had he failed to be there for me, he had now failed Cheryl as well. I was so angry at him because he wouldn't trust my concerns and do something. I blamed him for not acting earlier, rather than acknowledging that I could have done something myself."

Time only increased the distance between Sandy and Matt. Each grew more angry and more silent in their hurt. "One late night after Matt had been silent for quite a while, I asked him to tell me what was the matter. Eventually he told me he didn't think he loved me anymore. I wanted to know what I had done wrong and what I could do to change. It took a long time for what he said to sink in—that he didn't love me."

"During the next four months we began to talk—and we yelled a lot, too," Matt recalls. "What we said many times came out of 22 years of hurt and silence and anger. Things became very distorted. Finally we agreed we should go for counseling."

"The more we went, the more obvious it seemed to me that Matt was using this to make a probable divorce easier for the children," Sandy recalls. "I would not go for that reason, so we decided it would be best if we went separately. I hoped we could each work on our own issues and then start a new relationship.

"For a time I struggled with the changes I thought we needed to make in the marriage itself. I decided that if I affirmed Matt more, that would help. But he accused me of doing that only to get him to stay, and that I didn't mean it.

"Then I brought up everything I could remember that he had done to hurt or embarrass me. But the more I said, the worse I felt. After those discussions, I always felt like less of a person and more of an object to him."

"I could see that Sandy was trying," Matt said, "but it was too little, too late. Sometimes I set her up to make her angry and then ended by blaming her. Clearly we were both hurt, but we were both unwilling to really listen to the other. We kept pushing each other away with our words.

"I found it terribly trying to come home from a day of dealing with people, reaching out to others in my work, only to have to deal with a wife who gave me no peace and quiet. I have to admit she got better at giving me some space and that did make it a bit easier."

Sandy began to believe that Matt's intention was to leave the marriage. Her hopes came and went. One evening they went golfing as a family and seemed to have a lot of fun. Matt teased Sandy and even tried to show her how to hold a club. She felt as if there might be a chance after all. She told him how much she enjoyed the outing, but he informed her that although they did have a nice time together, it did not change his feelings for her and he intended to leave.

"I did not want a divorce, and I would not agree to one, but there was nothing I could do to change our relationship," Sandy concluded. "I had given him space and I was working on my issues, but now I needed to let go and accept that in Matt's eyes, the relationship was dead. I decided to let him leave if he wanted to."

When he actually prepared to leave, Sandy tried in various ways to make him feel guilty about it. "But I realized that his mother had used guilt all his life to get what she wanted, just like mine had. Matt had had it. I was behaving just like his mother.

"His leaving and my cold encounter with reality were probably the best things that could have happened then, although the next few days and weeks were terrible. The children kept me busy and life went on. I continued to become my own person, knowing that I loved Matt, but knowing, too, that I could no longer depend on him for my needs."

Telling the children about their decision was one of the most difficult things they had to do. The temptation to blame each other was great.

Sandy and Matt were to meet with an advisor to review financial issues, visitation rights and other matters that had to be addressed. Sandy had torn a ligament in her ankle and was on crutches. Matt offered to drive her to the meeting, but she was determined to be independent. However, he insisted.

The hours they spent going over the arrangements were difficult for both of them. On the way home Matt said with some hesitancy, "I really appreciate how you handled that tonight, Sandy. I felt you were willing to be fair with me."

Sandy was quite surprised, and even more unprepared when he asked if she would be willing to go to Recovery of Hope. Matt continued with sincerity, "While I was at the shore with my family, I discovered I still have some feelings for you. I don't understand them, but I would like to try."

"Inside I was doing all I could to stay calm," Sandy smiles, remembering. "I reminded Matt that we had both hurt each other, that we had both said a lot of angry things. Also, I was finally on my way to becoming an independent person and I didn't know if I was willing to risk being vulnerable again," she says. "I loved Matt, but I was a person of worth separate from him, and I wanted to continue to grow and mature into that person. Should I take the chance of being swallowed up in feelings of love and miss not dealing with the problems?" Sandy faced a true dilemma.

The next day was Cheryl's birthday. Matt had dinner with Sandy and the children, then took Cheryl golfing. When they returned, Matt seemed different to Sandy, more relaxed and at ease with them.

"Later that evening I took Sandy for a ride and told her that I loved her. I had come to those feelings on my own, without the help of anyone," Matt says with sincerity.

"It was about a month before we could register for Recovery of Hope," Sandy recalls, "and although we were happily getting to know each other and who we had become during the separation, I was apprehensive about going. We had begun to put some of our hurts behind us and I feared this might resurrect them all."

"The three hour session was an eye-opener," Matt recalls. "Amazingly, much of what was said related directly to our lives. I drove Sandy home and we talked for hours, something we had been unable to do before. We both decided to risk the hard work of a week of intensive therapy. It became a life-changing experience."

"I came to understand why my dad had such difficulty affirming me or anyone," Sandy says. "His three older brothers and sisters died before the age of two-and-a-half. His dad couldn't risk loving another son for fear of losing him. So my father had no example of how to love or affirm his children. He had never felt it himself.

"I found out my mother's parents had to get married, and my grandfather had to give up a wrestling career. He was an alcoholic who also molested his oldest daughter. No wonder I followed in their footsteps of hiding my feelings. My example had been one of secrecy. My mother never told me anything. I had to guess it.

"I learned my brother had a difficult time emotionally. I had not been told that he had a nervous breakdown, although I was scolded for being a terrible sister because I hadn't treated him in a caring way. How could I? I didn't know or understand what had happened. Secrets are powerful!"

Matt gathered new insights about why it is so hard for him to risk his feelings with anyone, or even to acknowledge that he has feelings. "It is not easy to change. Often I don't want to look at why and what I'm feeling, let alone express that to Sandy. I still feel quite vulnerable. But I know if we want a solid relationship, we will not take each other for granted or assume how the other feels," Matt concludes.

Matt and Sandy moved to a totally new area of the country and are, in a sense, starting over. Matt's job has put him in contact with many new people.

The move has been a bit more difficult for Sandy. She has spent hours making their new house a home, and is beginning to attend school functions and church activities, hoping to find new friends too.

Old patterns of relating are stubbornly hard to break. "Recently I tried talking to Matt abut becoming more involved in an adult class at church. I soon figured he wasn't interested because when I brought it up, he wouldn't make a comment," Sandy says. Rather than just let it go, she decided to pursue the conversation. "I would like to go to the adult class at church since I want a chance to make new friends," she told Matt.

To her surprise he said, "I wish you had said something last night. What about next Sunday?"

"I had assumed wrong," Sandy points out. "I put my feelings on the line, made myself vulnerable, and guess what? I was wrong. Matt *did* care and was willing to go with me."

It isn't always that easy. They both know they don't have to earn the love of the other, yet they still tend to respond that way to each other.

"Our anniversary last year was a hectic day," Sandy recalls. "I wanted us to do something special and we ended up at Matt's mother's. I was so disappointed and I began telling myself that Matt must not love me. But while we watched TV he gave me the most beautiful card. I had behaved like a child who had not gotten her own way!"

Matt remembers, too, how easily old patterns surface. "Right after we moved, I attended an all-day meeting—with both sets of car keys in my pocket! Sandy had asked me to leave keys so she could take Mark to his friend's birthday party. But I forgot."

"By the time I reached Matt, I was sure he had done it on purpose," Sandy confesses. "But he did run the keys back to me so I could take Mark to the party. He apologized when he came home, assuring me that he hadn't done it on purpose. I know that a set of keys had nothing to do with his love, but I still struggle with the need to be trusted. Next time I hope to be able to keep things in focus," Sandy sighs.

She continues to work long and hard at believing that she was not to blame for the painful incidents with her grandfather. "He used me just as the youth leader used our daughter—for his own distorted needs. I can choose not to take responsibility for what happened to me, despite the sound of my mother's voice which sometimes nearly convinces me otherwise.

"Matt has strengthened my trust in him and others by being trustworthy himself, and by affirming me and our relationship. It is clear to him that my broken trust with my grandfather hinders my ability to trust others, especially men. I had always felt safer caring about someone who didn't care about me so I wouldn't get hurt.

"My family of origin is a family of an alcoholic although no one in my immediate family drinks. Because Grandpa was an alcoholic, my mother belonged to the family of an alcoholic."

Matt continues, "In that respect, Sandy and I have had a double dose—my dad was also an alcoholic. Each of us had found ways of protecting ourselves from emotional hurt, most of them not very effective. I am learning to tune into my feelings, to trust them, to trust people and to feel worthy and entitled. Sandy loves me because of who I am, not for what I can do or not do. That's not always easy to remember."

Cheryl's abuse remains a sensitive issue between them. They fight not to blame each other for failing to sense the problem earlier.

"First I had to deal with my own anger and realize that it wasn't her fault or Matt's. Then I could allow Cheryl to work at her own pace through the difficult effects of having been molested by someone she trusted. Because of our mutual experience, we've been able to help each other toward healing," Sandy says with obvious care.

Matt and Sandy have grown closer as they've become more open with their feelings. "Now I ask Matt, 'Is something the matter or are you just enjoying the silence?' Whichever he answers, I have learned to accept either the silence or the chance to discuss what's on his mind," Sandy says.

Sandy may begin volunteer or salaried work in the area of abuse, "not because I need to prove myself, but because I want to," she explains, displaying some measure of her new self-understanding.

As they talk about their journey and their marriage, Matt observes, "We know now that no one person was at fault. We are products of our backgrounds and have often lived in response to them and not to each other. Our current task is to keep ourselves from falling back into old patterns, and instead risk continued openness with each other. We realize it's worth the struggle!" Sandy says emphatically.

17

Hope

Does one choose hope? Is it a decision one makes? Is it a gift? Or is hope inherent in one's personality—the optimist, for example?

Does hope require moving to a plane beyond reality so that one can claim what is not yet, but might be? Does it mean faith in the transcendent or in God?

Couples who have recovered hope, attest to the fact that hope is likely all of that, but is expressed in different ways for different persons. One may have a lot of hope for change and reconciliation, the other none. One may have hoped too often, had faith too often, only to be disappointed too many times to feel it is worth the risk of being hurt all over again. Others have prayed fervently that things would change and feel strongly that their faith has sustained them. Some have wondered about their faith in God who doesn't seem to answer.

The Recovery of Hope program is staffed by skilled therapists who employ a variety of assessment tools and clinical techniques. But what distinguishes Recovery of Hope is its premise that hope is contagious. By inviting despairing couples to hear the stories of couples who have reconciled, the program offers hope beyond commonly used counseling methods. Truthfully told stories are powerful. When joined with therapy that is intensely successive and relatively free of distractions, Recovery of Hope is able to assist couples in beginning again. The program emphasizes two areas that need particular attention by a husband and wife who are intent on creating a new relationship: acceptance and commitment.

Accepting one's spouse does not mean being resigned that she or he will never change. Instead of focusing only on one's spouse from a stance of criticism and blame, it first involves turning attention to self and owning personal responsibility for one's behavior and the need to change.

Further, "husbands and wives will discover that acceptance is not simply an endorsement of the status quo, but rather an acknowledgement that who you're married to is still someone you continue to love, despite his or her imperfections and difficulties in accommodating your wishes. The reward for the acceptor will be to discover that acceptance creates security and then change in the other person" (Kinder and Cowan: 217).

Beginning again is not returning to how things used to be. It does require finding new and satisfying ways to build a new marriage. It means acknowledging the commitment that was once made, but, at the same time, making a new one.

When two people marry, they are committing themselves to the confident prediction of what they will continue to feel for each other. That covenant applies as well to when they will not *feel* as much positive emotion for each other as they do at their wedding.

Each person changes. Differences emerge, expectations differ, self-interests are reasserted, and faults that had been overlooked or unacknowledged in the other can gradually become more focused and troublesome. As feelings change the relationship may be questioned. The marriage covenant, however, is an unconditional commitment that believes love can survive and grow through many changes. Anything less than a lifelong commitment is a contractual arrangement or agreement, not a marriage which lasts through the many changes that will inevitably come.

"When I married her, I thought she would always stay at home and be like my mom was. I thought she enjoyed all those domestic things. After all, she was a home-ec major and was really into that when we got married. Now she says she only did that to please her parents, that she always wanted to be a psychologist or something that allowed her to work with people who had difficulties. I didn't bargain for all this extra schooling and expense and me having to help with the housework. I can see how couples grow apart and feel like they've been betrayed," Marv says. "I know I've changed, too, and I'm committed to work at this with her, even if I don't always feel like it."

Dietrich Bonhoeffer, while imprisoned and awaiting his execution by Hitler's Gestapo, wrote a sermon for the wedding of two young friends. "It is not your love which sustains the marriage, but from now on the marriage which sustains your love." The original strong feelings which are so much a part of an early relationship, that feed each partner's personal, emotional and physical needs, tend to become less intense. But the marriage vows do not survive only as long as good feelings toward each other last. They are promises to God, for those whose faith asserts this, and to each other, for times when there are not feelings of great ecstasy and emotion. They continue, even when hope that was earlier so bright has all but disappeared.

Over time, intimacy and feelings of closeness come and go. Various stages of marriage have different stresses. Work, family, church and school activities, and financial pressures can so fully consume spouses that neither has a great deal of energy left for the other.

Distance and alienation can become so overwhelming, the chasm so deep, the accumulation of hurts and differences so profound, that couples may indeed wonder why they ever got married in the first place. They begin to believe that they chose the wrong spouse, that perhaps they weren't "made for each other" after all. They may feel that even though they promised to stay together for better or worse, it cannot get worse.

These couples frequently speak of having lost all hope of reconciling their differences. They come to a point of despair, believing they have no options for saving their marriages. Some are able to appeal to the commitments they made to each other. That can bring hope, however dim, for change.

Once revived, commitment can continue to sustain couples through the changes and the tensions that lie ahead.

Many couples who have lost hope have also lost their personal dreams as individuals. They may have given up their dreams for the sake of their marriages and families, both of which they consciously chose. Yet because of all the hurts their marriages have brought, they feel unfulfilled and even resentful in some unspoken or unacknowledged way. Some may never have allowed themselves to dream because so many of their hopes were disappointing or broken. But as a couple discovers new hope for a more satisfying wholeness in their marriage, their individual dreams and goals of what could be are also recaptured or newly born.

Nina talks about her early desires to be a teacher. "When I was a preschooler, my older brother and sister would sit at the table in the evening to do their homework and I would sit next to them pretending that I was in school. I loved to play school with them and whomever of the neighbor children I could persuade, and, of course, I always wanted to be the teacher. I expected perfection from my students! In school I was usually the girl at the top of the class, in constant competition with our neighbor boy George Kandle.

"I came from a very conservative farm family and my parents did not believe that higher education was necessary. Although I tried to persuade them to let me go to high school, I had to drop out when I was 15.

"I tried hard to fit into the social expectations of our family and church community. I met Paul, learned to love him, and when I was 19, followed the prescriptions set for me and married him. When we started in business together, I always kept the books, but I didn't know how to type. So I got a baby-sitter, took some typing classes and later a home-study accounting course. Despite having four children in five years, I was reminded of how much I missed school.

"Years went by. Our business became extremely successful. We traveled to all those places I had earlier only read about. But things were not going well in our marriage for a variety of reasons. Eventually we went for help. At one point the therapist asked me if I had a dream for myself that I had never fulfilled. I answered immediately, 'Yes, to go to school.'

"And I am doing it now. After finding resolution in our marriage, I was able to enroll in Frazier College. We moved from our old home place to a house just a few blocks from the college. Now Frank commutes to work while I study. He is pleased that I am finally doing what I've always dreamed about."

Another unexpected benefit of Recovery of Hope has been the development of Alumni Meetings. Although they were not part of the original therapy scheme, these get–togethers are held several times a year for couples who have experienced (benefitted through)the intensive week of therapy. They gather to support, encourage, laugh and cry together. At a recent such meeting, couples talked about changes they had made in various ways. Quite a few had changed jobs, were going back to school or beginning new vocations. Of the 21 couples attending that evening, 11 of them fit this category. Some were making a career switch because their earlier job interfered with their marriage. The majority, however, were following dreams, buoyed by the new life in their marriages.

Many couples who are reconciled acknowledge that they also experience a spiritual renewal and the strength that comes from that, whatever their faith community may be. Gordon MacDonald in his book, *Rebuilding Your Broken World*, describes this dynamic when he talks about "broken-world" people. He asserts that one cannot rebuild a broken world by trying to re-create life as though nothing had happened. Instead, one emerges from a very dark time with grace and humility, which one would not have had the difficulties never come.

"We broken-world people live with a strange irony," MacDonald says. "Not for one moment would we ever wish to repeat what caused the original collapse. But we cannot ignore the fact that when restoration has had its way, we may be in a better position to offer insight and grace to others than we ever were before" (MacDonald: 222-223).

Broken-world people are equipped to understand the pain and struggles of others because they know how it feels. Not only can they spot early signs of trouble in someone else, they are willing and especially able to help them in wise and caring ways because they have experienced brokenness.

That describes what Recovery of Hope is about. It is broken-world people, willing to share their stories of despair, hope, reconciliation and rebuilding. Because they are still in that process, they find meaning to the pain they have experienced as they share their stories. From that they also draw strength to continue the work of rebuilding.

Discovering and then telling one's story, along with experiencing brief but highly intensive marital therapy, are Recovery of Hope's first tools. Having undertaken that, most couples who continue with concerted effort, sound therapeutic principles, and hard work, can find mutual satisfaction in their marriages. The hundreds of couples who are Recovery of Hope alumni can attest to that.

Recovery of Hope
Network, Inc.

Program Centers and Directors
These centers welcome inquiries from couples interested in marital therapy. Comparable professional fees are charged for the week of intensive therapy. Scholarship funds are available, made possible by couples who have been helped by the program, through payroll deductions from employees of the centers who choose to contribute, from churches and other interested persons.

Recovery of Hope Network Office
Naomi and John Lederach, Directors
   283 S. Butler Road
   P.O. Box 550
   Mount Gretna, PA 17064
   1-800-327-2590

Adult and Family Life Ministry
   3501 S. Lake Drive
   Box 07912
   Milwaukee, WI 53207-0912
   (414) 769-3300

   Saturday sessions—Date/time change monthly. Call for information.

Catholic Social Services
   840 N. Grand
   Waukesha, WI 53186-4823
   (414) 547-2463

   Saturday sessions—Date/time change monthly. Call for information.

Eden Health Services
1844 Pembina, Suite 208
Winnipeg, Manitoba
CANADA R3T 2G2
(204) 275-6649
(204) 269-6543 FAX

Saturday sessions—Date/time change monthly. Call for
information.

Family Life Resource Center
2102 Port Republic Road
Suite C
Harrisonburg, VA 22801
(703) 434-8450

Saturday morning sessions—Third Saturday of January,
March, May, September, November.

Kings View
42675 Road 44
Reedley, CA 93654
(209) 638-2505
(209) 638-8279 FAX

Call for information and registration.

Oaklawn
2600 Oakland
Elkhart, IN 46517
(219) 533-1234
(219) 534-0157 FAX
1-800-282-0809

Saturday sessions—Second Saturday of each month.
Call for information and registration.

Philhaven
283 South Butler Road
P.O. Box 550
Mount Gretna, PA 17064
(717) 270-2447
(717) 270-2455 FAX

Saturday morning sessions—First Saturday each month except July.
Intensive week of Marital Therapy—Call for information.

Prairie View
2939 North Rock Road
Suite 100
Wichita, KS 67226
(316) 636-4344
(316) 283-2400 Newton

Saturday morning sessions—First Saturday each month except July and December (2nd Saturday).
Intensive week of Marital Therapy—Call for information.

Acknowledgements

This book contains true stories about real people. Each person, each couple, has given approval for their stories' publication. The stories are told, as nearly as possible, from the tellers' points of view. We have substituted different names, locations and circumstances in order to protect their identities.

These courageous people have expressed hope that through these stories, others may also receive hope. We acknowledge with deepest gratitude the willingness of each person and each couple to tell about their experiences so openly and vulnerably.

Our special thanks to Dr. Rowland Shank, Sr., whose foresight, interest, encouragement and commitment were highly instrumental in developing Recovery of Hope at Philhaven, as well as the National Network.

Gerald and Marlene Kaufman deserve special recognition for their initial interest in Recovery of Hope and the dreams they had for establishing the program in eastern Pennsylvania. They continue as co–therapists for the intensive week.

Dr. Steve Wilke, former president of Recovery of Hope Network, gave visionary leadership to the network that includes centers in many states and Canada.

To Marilyn Brooks belongs much credit for managing innumerable details on this book project as well as the Recovery of Hope program.

A final word. These stories touch familiar feelings in all of us. We cannot talk about *them* and *their* problems, but must also speak of *us* and *our* problems, since we deal with similar pain and joy, fear and faith, despair and hope. These are our common experiences. We are more alike than we are different.

Naomi and John Lederach
Philhaven
Mt. Gretna, Pennsylvania
Fall, 1991

Bibliography

Augsburger, David. 1988. *Sustaining love*. CA: Regal Books.

Beavers, W. Robert. January 1988. Attributes of a Healthy Couple. *Family Therapy Today*: 1–4.

Blau, Melinda. July/August 1990. Adult Children Tied to the Past. *American Health*: 57-65.

Bloomfield, Harold H. 1983. *Making peace with your parents*. NY: Random House.

Calof, David L. September 1988. Adult Survivors of Incest and Child Abuse, Part One: The Family Inside the Adult Child. *Family Therapy Today*: 1-4.

Hancock, Emily. 1989. *The girl within*. NY: E.P. Dutton.

Harley, Willard F. 1986. *His needs, her needs*. NJ: Fleming H. Revell.

Hendrix, Harville. 1988. *Getting the love you want*. NY: Harper and Row Publishers.

Krasner, Barbara R., and Joyce Austin. Winter, 1990. On Relational Ethics: Toward an Anatomy of Trust. *The Journal of Christian Healing*: 16-27.

Kinder, Melvyn and Cowan, Connell. 1989. *Husbands and wives*. NY: Clarkson N. Potter.

MacDonald, Gordon. 1988. *Rebuilding your broken world*. Nashville: Thomas Nelson.

Osborne, Philip. 1989. *Parenting for the 90's*. Intercourse, PA: Good Books.

Papp, Peggy. 1983. *The process of change*. NY: The Guilford Press.

Richardson, Ronald W. 1990. *Family ties that bind*. Vancouver: Self–Counsel Press.

Silverstein, Olga and Papp, Peggy. 1988. *The invisible web*. NY: The Guilford Press.

Smalley, Gary and Trent, John. 1986. *The blessing*. NY: Pocket Books.

Smedes, Lewis B. 1988. *Caring and commitment*. San Francisco: Harper and Row.

Smedes, Lewis B. 1988. *Forgive and forget—healing the hurts we don't deserve*. NY: Harper and Row.

Wangerin, Walter, Jr. 1990. *As for me and my house*. Kansas City: Thomas Nelson Publishers.

About the Authors

Naomi and John Lederach have been married since 1954. They are the parents of three children and have five grandchildren. They have spent 14 years in pastoral ministry and 16 years in teaching and administration at a private college.

Naomi has worked in the psychiatric/mental health field for over 24 years as an educator and nurse/therapist. She has a Master of Nursing degree from Wichita State University with a clinical emphasis in psychiatric/mental health nursing.

John has served as pastor, educator and therapist. He has a Doctor of Ministry degree from San Francisco Theological Seminary with a focus of study on the family. He has done additional study in Clinical Pastoral Education at Bowman-Gray School of Medicine, Winston-Salem, NC.

In September 1984, Naomi and John moved to eastern Pennsylvania to begin work with the Education Department and Recovery of Hope at Philhaven Hospital, Mount Gretna, PA. Philhaven is a private not-for-profit, comprehensive mental health care facility. They are currently co-directors of Recovery of Hope and the Recovery of Hope National Network.

They write for periodicals and journals, speak at conferences, retreats, professional meetings and church groups. They are featured on a five-part video series to help build and strengthen marriages and families titled "At-Home with The Family."